Ladies of Letters.com

Ladies of Letters.com

Carole Hayman and
Lou Wakefield

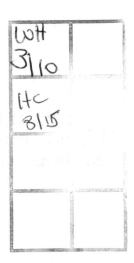

W F HOWES LTD

This large print edition published in 2002 by
W F Howes Ltd
Units 6/7, Victoria Mills, Fowke Street,
Rothley, Leicester LE7 7PJ

1 3 5 7 9 10 8 6 4 2

First published in 2001 by Warner Books

A CIP catalogue record for this book is available
from the British Library

ISBN 1 84197 523 0

Typeset by Palimpsest Book Production Limited,
Polmont, Stirlingshire
Printed and bound in Great Britain
by Antony Rowe Ltd, Chippenham, Wilts.

Foreword

Prisoner AG947
B Wing
HMP Lodley Grange
Lodley
Derbyshire

Dear Lou and Carole

Thank you for sending me the manuscript of 'Ladies of Letters.com'. I'm sorry not to have responded to it earlier, but it was confiscated on arrival, and has been sitting on Mrs Marmaduke, the governor's, desk ever since. She came to my cell and said, 'I am giving you permission to read this manuscript, Townsend, on the strict under-standing that your behaviour must improve. I hope you will not betray my trust.'

My cell mate, Fat Maggie, who can neither read nor write, asked me to read it aloud to her. I agreed, after she bribed me with five roll-ups and half a packet of Jaffa cakes. After a compul-sory lecture in the Education Department, on 'Empathising with The Victim', we returned to the cell, and I began the reading.

After a few pages Fat Maggie said, 'That Irene Spencer sounds like my bleedin' mum, an' she's the reason I'm in 'ere.' She continued to make many bitter interjections, until I threatened to stop the reading.

At 11.30am we went to the dining hall for lunch, and I took the manuscript with me as I was curious to know how Irene would fare in Melbourne. Frightening Freda and her gang came and sat at the same table, Freda demanded to know what I was reading. When I told her, her piggy eyes lit up. 'I've heard, "Ladies of Letters" on Radio 4,' she rasped. 'It were dead good.' She leaned across the metal tray which contained my fish fingers, boiled potatoes and mashed swede, and pulled the manuscript out of my hands. I knew better than to protest. Freda is the hardest woman in here, she's serving seven years for armed robbery. Though she claims it was not a gun she waved at the cashier in NatWest, but a deformed cucumber. For the rest of the day and long into the night, Freda's laughter could be heard reverberating around B wing.

In the morning, in the soap-powder queue, Freda said. 'That "Ladies of Letters.com" is the best fuckin' thing I've read since my divorce petition, you ain't 'avin' it back, Townsend.' Fat Maggie burst into tears, and begged Freda to relent, but Freda merely laughed harshly, pushed to the front of the queue and snatched more than her fair share of Persil. As she left the laundry room, she shouted, 'That Vera

Small reminds me of my mum, and she's the reason I'm in 'ere.'

I made a request to see the governor. Mrs Marmaduke listened to me sympathetically for once when I complained about Frightening Freda's theft of the manuscript. She said, 'I must confess Townsend, to having taken "Ladies of Letters.com" home with me, I did so enjoy Irene Spencer's and Vera Small's adventures. They both reminded me of my own mother. I will order Frightening Freda's cell to be searched immediately, and then arrange for Freda to be transferred to Holloway, providing that you ask your friends Lou Wakefield and Carole Hayman to send me signed copies of their published works for the prison library.' I had no option but to agree to these conditions, so, my dear friends, will you please grant me this favour. Incidentally, I come up before the parole board next month, though I am in a Catch 22 situation as I am still maintaining my innocence. There is a perfectly good reason why my garage contained a million Silk Cut cigarettes. I did not smuggle them in from France, I have been stockpiling them since hearing a rumour that cigarettes were to be banned by the Blair government.

Hope to see you on the outside soon.

Yours with Love,

Sue Townsend

Dear Irene,

I was going through some drawers in the Coach House yesterday and came across my old and dog-eared list of New Millennium resolutions. My first instinct, on reading 'must be more tolerant of Irene, she means well even though she is very trying', was to tear it into little, tiny pieces, but I found myself reading on and by the time I came to 'I will embrace my fellow man, with love and friendship', I was bathed in tears. I sat on the bed and howled. My veterinarian son-in-law St John said later he thought it was a poodle he'd just castrated. It brought back all the events of his and my daughter Karen's wedding day again. I haven't forgotten that I was left locked in the bathroom, while everyone else, including you, went off to Shagthorne Abbey without noticing, or that, while trying to climb out of the window, I impaled myself on the hook from which hangs the lavatory brush, and was shredded down to my undies. I will never forget the look on the bishop's face as the bride's mother staggered into the Abbey ripped and bleeding. Nor Karen's rage. As she said, or rather spat, at me,

1

during the reception, 'You'll do anything to draw attention to yourself, won't you Mother!' It was insult to injury when you accused me of being 'jealous of her happiness', especially since it was you who vacated the bathroom as I entered. Somebody turned the key in the lock, albeit absent mindedly.

However . . . the list made me think very hard about all the intentions I'd had of rising to the millennial challenge and it is in the spirit of that I offer you the chance to make amends. You'd better get a move on as I'm departing these shores for a trip to India. It was while I was searching for my sarong that I found my resolutions.

Yours, 'in love and friendship',

Vera

PS Before you take the 'embrace my fellow man' bit literally, let me assure you that I mean it in the biblical sense. I was not, as you suggested, practising with St John's charming young veterinary colleague at the reception, he was merely gaffer taping my splits. Apparently that's what they do now instead of stitching.

Dear Vera,

So glad you've reminded yourself of your New Year resolutions finally, albeit not until the summer months. In my experience, for most people, that's all they are – good intentions made while giddily intoxicated and kissing strangers, which are left to wither on the vine ere January is but a few days old. I have managed to remain faithful to my resolutions thus far this year, and I intend to continue in that vein, so I'm not going to be tempted by you into silly arguments about what did or did not happen at Karen's wedding. Suffice it to say that I am clear in my own mind that I played no part whatsoever in the sorry tale of you arriving in the Abbey in the middle of your only daughter's marriage ceremony with your skirt up around your ears and mouthing irreligious profanities.

I'm so glad to hear you've finally come out of your depression, though. Your daughter Karen has been in despair about you, and has often been on the telephone to me night and day since the wedding. I don't mind telling you that you had a close brush with homelessness around Easter, until I managed to calm her down and remind her that, though irritating beyond belief sometimes, you are nevertheless a very genuine person, and her mother.

I'm very pleased that you've obviously decided to take up your son-in-law St John's offer of a nice long holiday – I really do think that he and Karen need some quality time together alone, and that they both need to bond with your grandchildren Sabrina and Nelson in a way which is impossible with you around, given that you are so competitive for their affections.

I'm surprised you settled on India, however, given what you're like about toilet facilities – don't let it get you constipated like it did during our trip together in the Dormobile, especially not if you're going for several months as you've apparently promised Karen. I'm enclosing this jumbo box of senna as a going-away gift, and suggest you pack it near the top so you can start taking it straight away, before your phobias have a chance to take hold.

Have fun, old friend, and try to come back the richer for absorbing some of that wonderful Eastern philosophy – perhaps you might even learn some meditation out there, which I believe can be so helpful for people of an angry, impulsive nature.

I shall look forward to hearing all about your adventures in your cheery missives.

With warmth and compassion,

Irene

Dear Irene,

I shall ignore your ridiculous aspersions about 'kissing strangers' owing to shortness of time. But I must remind you, since obviously your brain is now a colander, that the bathroom incident was the culmination of 'words' about the catering. Not only did you criticise my use of sheep's yoghurt in the blue-cheese quiche, but you objected to the wilted dandelion in the salad and my own unique recipe for exotic lamb sausage. You said, if I remember correctly, fortunately my brain is not a colander . . . where was I . . . oh yes, that the sausage skin reminded you of an unpleasant object you hadn't seen for many a year. My poor son Howard was so hurt – you've no idea how many sheep he had to wrestle to get that length of intestine. He and his partner, Antony, were exhausted, despite the help of St John and his gaffer tape. Such a pity, as I was going to suggest we do a cookery book together, called, I thought, 'Two Fat Sausages'. Our recipes would go very well over the party season, I could see it stacking the shelves of Asda – but, never mind.

Thank you for the senna pods but they are

the last thing I shall need in India. I'm assured curry works on a level similar to colonic irrigation. I am not, by the way, going for 'several months', whatever Karen has told you, but on a three-week guided tour with an exciting new enterprise called Gaga. They specialise in adventures for the elderly, and had we been speaking, I would have asked you to come too. Though on second thoughts, you'd probably be happier with a quiet saunter in Bognor. St John, who is the most thoughtful and generous of son-in-laws, offered me a holiday months ago. But I haven't had a moment, what with the renovations at The Bothy (Karen has spent a fortune on so-called 'architects', and what's left of the house is held up by scaffolding), helping out Howard and Antony at the sheep farm and looking after Sabrina and little Nelson.

I do wonder what Karen is thinking of, getting herself pregnant again so quickly. She's already blown up like a barrage balloon, which can't be wise in the first year of a marriage. Sabrina, poor little thing, has sobbed herself to sleep every night for a week, at the thought of being separated from her Granny. I told her I'd be back in time to see her new little brother or sister born, but that just made her cry louder.

All 'til I'm in touch with foreign parts,

Vera

42 The Limes
Hethergreen

Dear Vera,

I know you're just about to leave these shores but I really must clear up some of your misapprehensives before you go.

1. Blue Cheese Quiche is made with blue cheese. If it were otherwise it would be named otherwise. Personally I would anticipate very little demand for an item named 'Sheep's Yoghurt Quiche', let's say.

2. The dandelion leaves in question were not 'wilted', they were deceased.

3. *You* said the sausage skin reminded you of an unpleasant such-and-such. I merely added that I wouldn't know as I had not personally seen one. Ever. Clive and I preferred to keep some mystery in our marriage. However, if you are thinking of 'connecting with foreign parts', as you write in your last, I only hope that you have packed plenty of the things that sausage skins remind you of.

4. If you are considering writing a book called 'Two Fat Sausages', I suggest you find another more suitably sized writing partner. I personally have never been anything but a size 12.

With sincere best wishes for a very pleasant holiday,

Irene

42 The Limes
Hethergreen

Dearest Karen

It was lovely to talk to you on the phone last night, and I'm so pleased you're happier now that your Mum has gone off to India and given you some breathing space. Of course I don't mind coming over to help out with Sabrina and Nelson. I've found out about the trains as arranged – could you or St John pick me up at Great Shagthorne station at 1.03 on the 23rd? I am busy organising things here so that I can stay for as long as you need me, so don't worry about a thing.

So looking forward to seeing you all.

Fondest love,

Rene

TUESDAY · DARJEELING ·

St John and Karen

The Coach House Apartment

The Bothy

Long Lane

Little Shagthorne

Great Britain

Dear St John and Karen,

Sorry to be brief, but tour bus impounded by police after nasty incident. Pig on the road. Animal, I mean, not driver. Rescued by charming Indian taxi driver, who drove me the rest of the way. 675 miles. Now completely out of rupees. Staying with taxi driver. Wire money to State Bank of India, Darjeeling.

Love,

Vee/Mother

Sabrina
The Coach House Apartment
The Bothy
Long Lane
Little Shagthorne
Great Britain

Dear Sabrina,

Hope you like the postcard of the mosque. Granny's only seen it from the outside, too. Women aren't allowed in. Missing you terribly, but have been adopted by several cats, dogs and goats. Oh, and a pig. We're all staying with a helpful taxi driver and his large family. The weather is freezing. Just as well, as with all of us in one room, it's very cosy!

Have bought you a sari and lots of jewels. Bet you can't wait to have me back.!

Big kisses and a cuddle for Nelson (not too tight, remember he's only a baby).

All my love,
Granny

Irene Spencer

42 The Limes

Hethergreen

Great Britain

Dear Irene,

Thought you'd enjoy this ethereal vista of the Himalayas. So different from the flatness of Hethergreen. I went up to 8,000ft yesterday, hanging on to a cable car. Actually I was hanging on to it from below, having slipped out as I leant over to take a photo. Marvellous view of the tea estate!

No trouble with the other "down below", food wonderful! Sheep's yoghurt in everything. And other parts of its anatomy. Now thinking of travel cookbook. "Vera's Voyages". On my own, naturally.

Vera

11

Dear Howard,

Enc'd is a p.c. of Darjeeling's 'toy train'. Isn't it
sweet? It struggles up the mountain puffing hard,
rather like you on your bike in Great Shagthorne.
You would love it here. It's very oldie-worldie
English. Just like the books I used to read you
when you were little. There's lots of falling-down
colonial houses. And falling-down colonial people.
Gin is very cheap. Really, nothing seems to have
changed since the last century. There's a tea shop
(Darjeeling tea, naturally) where I go every afternoon to write my postcards. It's called
Glengoolie's and is decorated with stag bits and
tartan. Have met a lovely couple of boys there,
Raj and Shiva, who remind me so much of you
and Antony. They are a great giggle. They are
'tourist guides' and tonight they are taking me to
the Planter's Club, for its speciality, (you guessed
it) Gin Fizzes! It's terribly posh and I shall have
to dress up. I'm thinking of trying out my new
sunset-flame-coloured sari. No idea how to wrap
it! Will have to get Raj to model it for me.

Love and kisses to you both,

Mumsie

The Coach House Apartment
The Bothy
Long Lane
Little Shagthorne

Dear Vera,

Surprise! Here I am, tucked up in your bed at Karen and St John's beautiful home, early on a lovely English summer's morn, with your little granddaughter Sabrina nestled at my side, while we write to Granny Small. Sabrina is such a dear, isn't she, and *so* affectionate! She sends her Big Love to you, and the enc 'dawring' of she and I picking flowers in Shagthorne Wood, which we did together yesterday – the flat is *filled* with flora, which has helped enormously to mask the terrible smell that greeted my nostrils when I first arrived. Karen and I searched high and low for its origin on my first day here, and neither one of us could come up with a plausible explanation, once we'd found the smoked mackerel, as to what on earth could have been going on in your mind when you pushed it down the back of the sofa. Any clues forthcoming? Anyway, in case you're wondering why I'm here, Karen rang me just after you'd left, asking if I could spare time to help look after Sabrina while you are away and she is so heavily pregnant – Karen, that is, not your granddaughter! Naturally I was only too delighted to help out, and will remain here as long as I'm needed, so don't even think of being obliged to me – it is entirely my pleasure that your family feel so comfortable with me that they can ask for my help.

All your postcards arrived in a rash over the last few days incidentally – even mine, which was sent on to me from The Limes by my neighbour Beryl, who is popping in and out to water the plants, etc. I went over for dinner to your son Howard and his partner Antony's last night – gosh it was fun, and the food was superb – not a drop of sheep's yoghurt anywhere – and so beautifully presented! Instead of the usual white paper frills on the end of the cutlets, Antony had tied bows of ribbon in all the colours of the rainbow – I had blue and orange while 'The Boys' fought over the pink and purple. All in jest and good humour, of course. They really are lovely, and they seem so happy together – they're almost like a married couple, aren't they?

I hope you manage to get this, c/o the State Bank of India, Darjeeling. Don't you have a Post Restaurante address over there? It would be so nice to be able to keep you informed of your family news on a more regular basis. Or we could even 'e-mail' each other – St John has been showing me round 'The World Wide Web' on his computer and it really is a marvel! He's given me my own e-mail address while I'm here

– irene@littleshag.com – which is lovely, but a bit frustrating until I get some correspondents. St John says that there are Internet Cafés all over the world now, so if you can find one in Darjeeling, have a go, Joe!

All for now, as it really is time we got up. Young children have such a small attention span, don't they, and Sabrina is complaining that 'writing to Granny is boring now' – such a delightful child, and what a sense of humour! Hope to hear from you soon, and that ideas for your new solo recipe book are coming thick and fast.

Warmest wishes,

Irene

Dear St John,

Thank you so much for the money transfer, which arrived in the nick of time. I was about to take to the street with my begging bowl, like so many of the other residents of Darjeeling. They are a picturesque lot in their rags, though I wouldn't go so far as to have anything amputated. I can also pay my bill at the Planter's Club, where I apparently ordered 32 Gin Fizzes! You really are a dear, and the best son-in-law any mother could wish for. How is Karen, by the way? I hope the pregnancy is progressing well and she has got over that deafening heaving and retching and returned to her normal colour.

It's very cold in Darjeeling and, thanks to you, I've been able to move into a hotel with a stove and buy a blanket wrap (high fashion here) and fur hat. It looks like a National Health wig, but at least it keeps my ears warm. With the help of the local Chief District Commissioner for Train Reservations (such a nice man, loved my pineapple-sag-aloo recipe) I've secured a place to Calcutta and a flight home on the 21st. Sabrina and Nelson must be pining for me and

I wouldn't miss Karen's confinement for the world. The thought of her going through all that agony without her mother present!

Incidentally, I've had a very odd letter from Irene. I know she is staying with you but she also seems to have 'borrowed' my identity. If I don't return soon, she'll have taken to wearing my clothes and calling herself 'Vera'.

I hope you're impressed with my e-mail skills. My dear new friends, the boys Raj and Shiva, introduced me to the Jasmine Cybernet Café. They said it was high time I joined the World Wide Web, and, besides, I'd be able to keep in touch with them.

See you all on the 21st. I'd be grateful, dear, if you could meet me at the airport. I've purchased so many lovely things in the bazaars, I've had to get two more bags to carry them.

All my love to you and the children. And Karen of course,

Vera

Dear Irene,

Recipe no. 1 – Sag Aloo with Pineapple

2lbs aloo
1 lb sag
1 pineapple
4 cardomum
1 tspn garam masala
1 tspn coriander
half kg sheep's yoghurt

Stew aloo in ghee until soft. Add sag, cubed pineapple and spices and stir vigorously. After 2 or 3 mins add yoghurt and serve with fresh chapati.
Please pass on to Howard and Antony.

Your first cyberpal,

Vera

PS The smoked mackerel will have been my pit bull terrier, Rex. He's such a dear, always hiding little 'offerings' for me. I once found a headless ferret in the biscuit tin. I can only pray it was one of St John's veterinary specimens.

Dear Vera,

Well, here I am on my inaudible trip on the
World Wide Web, and I have to say it seems
very like common-or-garden typing to me! Did
I ever mention that's what I did before I was
married? Actually, I wasn't a typist in a pool – I
was personal secretary to Mr Blundell, the
Managing Director of Fairweather Feet, a very
well-respected firm that made quality wellington
boots and galoshes. I am astonished to say that
I appear to have lost little of my skill in the
intravenous years, and all ten of my digits are
happily finding their way to the right keys, if a
little more slowly than hitherto. Ha Ha! St John
has just suggested that I do some office work
for him, now he's discovered my latent talent!
Such a shame that *you* didn't learn an office
skill when you were young, otherwise you could
help him out when you are home, and pay off
some of the debt you apparently now owe him.
What was it you used to do? Wasn't it factory
work of some kind, or were you a shop girl? I
half remember some rambling tale you told me
once when you were 'in your cups', about your
mother telling you you'd be 'one of Woolworths''

if you didn't apply yourself harder at school.

Speaking of school, I went with Sabrina to her 'Bring-A-Granny' Event at Shagthorne Junior yesterday, since you weren't here. It's a new innovation to bring history alive for the little dears, hearing it at first hand. Sabrina was so happy I could go with her, and was so proud of my story-telling skills – I told them all about rationing and Woolton Pie, and afterwards the catering staff begged me for the recipe. Happily, also, Mrs Patel was there from the Filcham Magna Corner Store, so I asked her if she knew what 'Sag' and 'Aloo' were. Honestly! If you mean 'potatoes' and 'spinach', I don't know why you don't just come out and say it. Sabrina said it sounded 'orribill' – she's such a caution! Nevertheless, as soon as it was home-time, we trundled over to her Uncle Howard's to give him the recipe, since you made such a song and dance about it, and he cooked it straight away, substituting Cox's Orange Pippins for the pineapple, as naturally, here in the Derby Dales we do not have access to exotica except in tins, and you know what Howard is like about fresh produce. All of us thought it was highly over-rated – Sabrina actually said it was 'pukey', and demonstrated her feelings in the back of the MG Midget when Howard was kind enough to drive us home. She's going to sleep with Granny Irene tonight to make her feel better.

Well, all for now, old friend. So glad you're

enjoying yourself. Karen is blooming. Sabrina says hello, and please can you bring her 'an heffalump' (we're reading 'Winnie The Pooh'). Nearly forgot, you had a visitor the other evening – Edward Blunt? Says you met at the Parish OAP Beetle Drive last winter, and was inviting you to another this weekend. I told him you were away, so he insisted on taking me instead. You are a dark horse – he's quite attractive in a rough and ready rural sort of way, isn't he? Will tell you all about it in my next.

Fond regards,

Irene

The Coach House
The Bothy
Long Lane
Little Shagthorne

My Dear Irene,

I'm so sorry to have missed you. I was expecting a warm reunion – indeed the hot water bottle in my bed *was* still warm – but Karen told me you had taken off 'like a bat out of hell' on hearing some news from home. I do hope it's nothing serious. I couldn't help wondering what on earth you were doing at Little Shagthorne when your own daughter Lesley is pregnant and your own grandchild Cheryl Marie must be feeling very neglected. Of course, St John filled me in about your rift with Lesley after she'd refused to have you over to Oz, and how you'd suddenly descended here out of the blue. They said you were distraught and how sorry they felt for you. Unfortunately, those sympathies don't last if one outstays one's welcome.

It looks like I've arrived home in the nick of time. Karen's about to burst at the seams – which reminds me of India – and Sabrina's complaining you 'smelled funny' (ditto). Out of the mouths of babes! I'm sure she's only refer-ring to your 'tea-rose' cologne, which I've always thought rather vinegary. She's such a little performer. She's parading around with a turban on her head and has set up a stall on The Bothy building site, with the jewellery I brought her. She's already sold a hod full of plastic bangles to one of the bricklayers. She's saving up for a mountain bike. Everything else is forgotten!

Must stop now. Nelson is crawling into my Indian trunk and he's not too old for a cot death. I've got an avalanche of mail to answer! The postcard I sent my son Howard and his partner Antony didn't arrive until this morning – I could have saved an hour in the queue at Darjeeling post office and flown it over myself! It was of the stunning Millennial dawn over Kanchenjunga – they were still selling like hot cakes there, all these months later. Howard said it was all right, but didn't compare to sunrise over Great Shagthorne.

Drat it, Edward Blunt's coming up the drive. I hope *he* isn't expecting a warm reunion.

Namaste, (ask Mrs Patel for a translation)

Vera

My Dear Karen and St John,

I am sending this note hand-delivered by Mr Blunt, as he has kindly offered to pick up my other suitcase from you and drive it back over to me at The Limes. Sorry to leave in such haste as to make myself so forgetful but, as you know, my neighbour Beryl made it all sound so dramatic that I simply had to leave immediately and come and see for myself. I have to tell you, thus far I've drawn a complete blank, so I'm none the wiser. Certainly no 'strange man' seems to be watching the house now, and I've been peeping out from behind the curtains ever since I arrived back yesterday afternoon. And there's no sign of a forced entry and nothing seems to be missing, except, of course, the mysterious disappearance of the contents of my dustbin, as reported by Beryl to me when she phoned me at your lovely home, The Bothy. Naturally I've put the Hethergreen West Neighbourhood Watch on full alert, but I can only imagine that it was just children having a lark. Which doesn't explain the Mystery Man staking out the house, but then Beryl is prone to fervid over-imaginings sometimes (she used to be a leading light in the Hethergreen Amateur Dramatic Society, or HAMS, as it is known to officionados, and I think she misses the drama).

Anyway, my dears, please give my suitcase to Mr Blunt, and accept what I hope is the lovely box of chocolates he has selected for you on my behalf. It was an absolute pleasure helping out with the little ones, and you needn't think twice about asking me again.

Hope Vera arrived back safely. Give her my love, and tell her we'll catch up on all our news soon.

Fondest love,

Irene xxxxx

PS And an extra special 'Granny Spencer Huggle' for my darling Sabrina XOX

Dear Irene,

A quick note, which I'll pop in with the suit-case and bag Edward is bringing. I found sundry articles of yours – how long have you been using the truss? – dotted all over, so have collected them all into this gorgeous, hand-crafted Rajastani bag. Do feel free to keep it, I've got lots more. It wouldn't have been my first choice as a present for you, a little too bold with its colourful stripes and mirrors. In fact I'd brought you a lovely, pure silk scarf – the trouble I had finding beige – but that seems to have got mixed up with the tandoori-chicken powder and has turned a magical shade of terracotta – so remi-niscent of the earth in India – and I think it's more me than you now, so I'll hang on to it.

I'm so glad Edward's removing your suitcase, which I fell over several times. Whatever possessed you to bring such a big one? You must have thought you were moving in! Now, at last, I can unpack all my treasures. I'm going to completely re-do The Coach House 'Indian' style and have brought back lots of hangings in shades of saffron, tangerine and magenta, the colours worn by the Buddhist monks I encountered (photo enclosed – that's the chief llama holding the football).

I passed your note on to Karen and St John once I realised it was for them. Edward had given it straight to me so, of course, I couldn't help reading it . . . (He's well meaning enough but a simple soul. I do hope he isn't delivering your stuff in his poultry van – last time he gave me a lift in that, I came out smelling like an Indian loo and covered in chicken feathers.) It sounds as though Beryl isn't the only one who misses 'drama'. Why on earth would a mystery man be lurking about your house and rifling the contents of your dustbin? That sort of thing only happens to soap stars and television presenters. You haven't won the lottery and not told us?

Anyway, I do hope whatever the problem with Lesley, you've made it up now.

Edward is gobbling like one of his turkeys, so I'll finish.

Thanks for the chocolates, by the way. 'Quality Street' is an unknown concept in India. All the roads are absolutely disgraceful.

I'll write properly and send you more pictures of my adventures, as soon as I'm settled. What a good thing St John installed the computer. Must 'log on' and e-mail all my new pals on the subcontinent!

All the best,

Vee

Dearest Irene,

Thanks for your letter, which Mother eventually gave me. I'm glad you're OK and of course you're welcome here any time. Though where we'd put you I don't know, what with The Bothy still being a building site, and needing a nursery for the new baby and a suite for the nanny I'm insisting St John hires . . .

Mother's got boxes and trunks everywhere, she's turning The Coach House into a Bedouin tent. There's carpets and cushions and yak-skin rugs. St John says we'll have to re-name it The Shag Palace. Even Howard said the colours made him feel bilious, though that could have been the curry she insisted on feeding him. She's trying out all her new recipes. If she sends you the one for mutton masala, don't touch it!

Love,

Karen

Dear Vera,

Have just received your nasty letter in the post. I don't know what you think you stand to gain from fabricating lies about a rift between myself and my daughter Lesley. We are, in fact, the best of friends, and as close as a mother and daughter can be when one lives in England and the other lives in Australia. In fact, we are both currently looking into our finances to see if we can afford for me to fly out again to Melbourne to be with her during her confinement. As for outstaying my welcome with your daughter Karen and her husband St John, all I can say is Ha! – you should have heard what they were saying about *your* eminent return before you go throwing stones in glass houses – your ears would have spontaneously combusted.

Edward has also delivered your note to me this morning, which I read out to him, so now he knows what you say about him and his poultry van behind his back. He says you can forget free cocks from him from now on, and can go out and buy them yourself. The truss, incidentally, is his. It's a long story, and not one I would want to go into with such an antipathetic co-respondent such as yourself, but suffice it to say that we thoroughly enjoyed ourselves at the Beetle Drive and got on like a house on fire – as in fact I seem to do with all your friends and family.

Must go – there's a policeman at my door. *You* may think my dustbin being plundered is a joke, but I am happy to say that here in Hethergreen it is sufficiently out of the ordinary to arouse the interest of the CID.

Kind regards,

Irene

PS Almost forgot. Welcome home.

Dear Irene,

Forgive this scribble but Mother's got all the
computer equipment in her room and I'm far
too huge and heavy to drag myself there. This
painting by Sabrina is all I've got to hand.
Ignore the dark red blotches. I don't know what
you've been telling Ma. She's accusing us of
saying nasty things behind her back and trying
to get rid of her. It seems to stem from a
misunderstanding about why you were here. I'm
afraid it's my fault, I let it drop that you'd
planned a long visit to Oz, but your daughter
Lesley had refused to pay for your flight, and
you were so upset we asked you over.

Also, our neighbour Edward Blunt the poultry
farmer hasn't spoken to her since he came for
your stuff. You should know that they were
'seeing' each other for a while, but fell out over
her attempts to re-educate him. She kept buying
him Classic FM tapes to listen to on his
delivery rounds. He said he felt a fool playing
'William Tell' to a van full of squawking
chickens. When she gave his favourite tweed
jacket to Little Shagthorne 'Help The Aged',
saying it made him look like Worzel Gummidge,
it was the final straw (no pun intended). In a

31

village it's a bit bloody awkward, so we sent her away on holiday.

She's now taken to her bed with what she says is 'a touch of malaria'. My husband St John's taken her temperature and says it's only a cold, but she's swathed in a mosquito net and demanding quinine. St John's up to his elbows in a difficult hysterectomy. The way I'm feeling, I may book myself in for the next one. Sabrina's sulking, Nelson's teething, Rex is whining. I just can't deal with this in my present condition. The only good thing is that Ma's temporarily stopped cooking. Her last effort in the kitchen (curried brains – her own, judging by her recent behaviour) nearly brought on premature labour!

For goodness sake, do whatever you can to smooth things over,

All the best,

Karen

PS Forgot to ask what the police make of the dustbin situation. Have they considered foxes?

42 The Limes
Hethergreen

My Very Dear Karen,

Thank you for your note, and for darling little Sabrina's painting. The red blotches do make it look rather 'disturbed' – has she painted it since her Granny Vera's been back? Poor little mite. We got on so well – she used to cling to me like a limpet when I was staying with you and we had our cuddles – so I suppose she must be really missing me. Doubly so, if her real Grandmother has turned nasty. (What am I saying – 'turned'? What you have to put up with from your Mother!)

Anyway, it's nothing new to me. How our 'relationship' has survived thus far I sometimes fail to comprehend. But I am not one to bear grudges, as you know, so I'm enc-ing a letter for She Who Must Be Obeyed, to try to smooth things over, as you suggest.

Try to rest, dear. In your condition you can't be too careful. My one regret is that I couldn't have stayed to see you through the birth. I hope you've changed your mind about the 'Home Delivery' now Vera's back – she'd only interfere.

Tons of love and kisses for you, Big Huggles for Sabrina and Nelson (by the by, have you tried my suggestion of rubbing rum on his little gums yet to help with the teething?). And a special kiss for St John.

Irene

PS I was a bit puzzled about you telling Vera that you invited me over because you felt sorry for me, since you and I both know that you begged me to come – but I suppose you decided on a white lie to make her feel better. Anyway, hope the enc. does the trick to turn her mood around . . .

Dear Vera,

Karen tells me you're poorly with a slight cold. I hope you aren't being a nuisance to her while she is so heavily pregnant – she must be exhausted, poor lamb. To relieve your symptoms I recommend boiling up some cloves with lemon juice and honey, and if you want to push the boat out, mix in some whisky. It works for me.

No doubt now you are back from the subcontinent you are feeling a bit flat, but life can't all be one long holiday. Do feel free, however, to write to me, telling me of your adventures, if it will help cheer you up.

My news is that the Hethergreen police have drawn an absolute blank so far on the Mystery Man who stole the rubbish from my dustbin. I am inclined now to believe it must have been a starving homeless person, or, as your daughter Karen suggested, maybe a fox. However, Beryl-next-door still swears there was a man 'staking out' my house while I was away – in fact she still has nightmares about him. Looking at the sketch she did in order to assist police with their enquiries, I am not surprised, but then again perhaps that is due to her drawing skills – or lack of them. Speaking of which, your gorgeous little granddaughter Sabrina just sent her Granny Spencer a lovely drawing of dark red splodges and something that looks like a meat cleaver sticking out of somebody's head. Hope you haven't been reading Grimms' Fairy Tales to her again – she has such a vivid imagination!

Hope you are feeling better by the time this arrives, and are being less of a drain on poor Karen's scant resources, energy-wise.

Much love,

Irene

Dear Irene,

Haven't got time to write to you about adventures as I am busy preparing a lecture on them for Great and Little Shagthorne Geographical Society. They've begged me to fill their 'Traveller's Tales' slot with a commentary and slides. It's a great honour, which I shall have to work night and day to fulfill, especially as I've also offered to do the refreshments. I thought it would be a good opportunity to try out some of the recipes I'm including in my cookbook, 'Vera's Voyages'. I've had to scour the World Wide Web for ingredients. You can't get anything exotic in the Derby Dales, as my son Howard is always saying. Though having seen his partner Antony draped in the purple striped 'lungi' I brought him back, I don't know why he's complaining.

I haven't got a cold, it's a recurrence of malaria – it can dog travellers for years, as you'd have no occasion to know. Whisky is the last thing you should take with quinine – though come to think of it, gin wouldn't be so bad – but I always find the best cure, feverish though I am, is to be up and active. Sabrina, little angel, has been helping me by 'designing' my 'Traveller's Tales' programme. I told her all about the Goddess Kali and her bloodthirsty ways, which may be the origin of the meat cleaver. I couldn't help noticing that her severed heads have an uncanny resemblance to yours, but it's probably coincidence.

Must get on, I'm doing a trial run of Gobi Manchurian tonight, which Howard and Antony are coming to sample. I've enc'd an invite to the 'Do' on Tuesday, though it's too short notice for you to be able to come.

I'm sure Karen would send love if she wasn't asleep, and Sabrina, if she remembered.

Yours,

Vera

Great and Little Shagthorne Geographical Society

cordially request your presence at

Vera Smalls' vibrant and entrancing account of her voyage through India.

Followed by

A Reception to Launch her Collection of Oriental Recipes.

An evening wonderfully evocative of

the sights, the sounds, the tastes, the smells of India.

42 The Limes
Hethergreen

Dear Vera,

I'm so glad I managed to get to your
Geographical Society 'Do', despite the short
notice you gave me. It was just luck that
Edward Blunt was staying over here at The
Limes when the invitation arrived, so we simply
leapt into the van, drove like maniacs up the
motorway, and 'Bob's Your Uncle', as the saying
goes (I wonder why?). Anyway, as we had to
drive straight back afterwards I didn't manage
to congratulate you on your 'efforts', which, as
far as I could hear from where I was sitting in
the second row, were sterling, despite the hecklers. Who were they? Did you know them? And
what do they have against you, exactly? I don't
care what they shouted, I thought you looked
really interesting in that sari. Would you call
that colour puce? As for your cooking demon-
stration – well, what can I say? It certainly lived
up to your promise of 'the smells of India'.

I don't know if you noticed, but I struck up
quite a conversation with Alan Bagshaw, the
Geog. Soc. President, during your interval, and
he's begged me to give a lecture on my
Australian travels. He wanted me to do it the
week after next, but what with expecting my
daughter Lesley to send me a panic message at

any moment to go to Melbourne and assist with her birth, I thought it more prudent to put it off a while longer. And it will be better in the long run anyway – my Australian news will be hot off the press!

I hope that Howard and Antony are over their biliousness now. Any idea what caused it? Do give them my love. And love as always to your daughter Karen (who looked blooming!), to dear St John and baby Nelson and, of course, to Granny Irene's little Sabrina.

Best wishes to you too, dear,

Irene

Dear Irene,

I suppose I should thank you for making the effort to attend my occasion, but really, what with your late arrival, insistence on clambering over my audience just when I'd got them totally enthralled and Edward Blunt's cellphone going off and him having a loud argument about foulpest during my poignant description of the cremation ghats at Varanasi, it would have been better if you hadn't! The hecklers, by the way, were telling Edward to shut up. Except for the one who was kindly pointing out that I'd inadvertently hitched up the back of my sari. It must have been when I dashed to the loo with pre-show nerves. Fortunately my undies were in the same shade of flamingo. The moment was only saved by the elemental magic of fire. As 'A Fan' commented afterwards, they could almost smell the bodies burning. Actually that turned out to be the dratted projector, which Alan Bagshaw insisted he'd had mended. He's very forgetful, I'm afraid – there's a move in the society to get him declared unfit for office.

Several of the audience asked afterwards who on earth was the woman with the hysterical laugh. I explained – with my face the same colour as my sari – that you were, or had been, a 'friend'. I got some old-fashioned looks, I can tell you. At least one person suggested your behaviour was deliberate sabotage. It kept me awake all night wondering if that was true. Why, Irene, why? Jealousy, I suppose. I've got a lovely life in a lovely home with a loving son-in-law and grandchildren. You've got . . . Edward Blunt.

I do hope you'll ponder on this and decide not to let the green-eyed monster triumph. We used to be such pals.

Yours in sorrow,

Vera

PS There were a couple of publishers at the 'Do', acquaintances of Howard and Antony. They're starting up their own 'list' on the Internet. Cookery books are apparently big sellers! They were so astonished by the taste of my 'Bhindi Bhaji', I said I'd send them a 'proposal'.

My Dear Vera,

Flabbergasted would not be too strong a word
to describe my feelings on reading your last,
and that only since I put a drop of rum in my
coffee to calm me down. Pre this old-fashioned
remedy, I was running the gamut of emotions
from Deepest Hurt to Violent Outrage.

What more do you want of my friendship? I
feel I've given all I have to give. *You* go frol-
icking off to India; *I* go to your home to look
after your family. *You* feel poorly; *I* send an old
family recipe for the cure. *You* send me a tardy
invitation to a lecture you're giving; *I* move
heaven and earth to be there to wish you well.
If you weren't far too long in the tooth, I'd
think you were going through The Change Of
Life.

As you know, I always make a fair copy of my
letters, valuing neatness as I do, so I have
trawled through the rough draft of my last
missive a million times, trying to find a sliver of
a reason for your hideous accusations, and can
find none. *Me* jealous? Of *you*? It would be
laughable if it weren't so wounding. I wonder if
the boot isn't on the other foot, and that *you*
are in fact jealous of *me* – or rather, of my
friendship with Edward, who, I hear, you made

several embarrassing attempts to seduce. Or jealous of my warm and loving relationship with your daughter Karen, who, I notice, was not included when you were counting your blessings in the poison pen you sent me.

Think long and hard about this before replying, and when you do, post it care of St Urbans, Melbourne, for – and here's something else you might be jealous of – my daughter Lesley has sent me an air ticket and entreated me to fly halfway round the world to be with her for the birth of my second grandchild.

Yours in tiny little pieces,

Irene

PS Not that you'd be interested, but a strange man who looks just like Beryl-next-door's sketch of the man who was staking out my house when I was away, followed me round Tesco's yesterday. I managed to lose him in Feminine Hygiene, but it has left me feeling very vulnerable and glad to be going away again. But don't, whatever you do, feel worried on my account.

Dearest Lesley,

I've been looking at my finances and found that if I'm very careful for the rest of the year, I can in fact afford to come over to Australia to help you with the birth, and to look after my darling little Cheryl Marie. I've bought my ticket today and will be arriving on Sunday.

With all my love, dear,

Mummy xx

PS Love to Brian. Any news yet about his divorce so the two of you can get married? It would be so unfortunate if the new little one were to be born out of wedlock.

The Coach House Apartment
The Bothy

Dear Irene,

Oh for the days of telegrams! Or if only you
had e-mail! Can't bear you to fly halfway round
the world in Violent Outrage. It would only give
you flatulence and nothing is worse on a
cramped plane, as I know from personal experience.

I do hope this note reaches you in time. I've
enclosed a photo of us which is one of my
favourites – arms linked, squinting into the sun.
If I remember rightly it was taken in Capri by a
gentleman who invited me to the casino. You
insisted afterwards he was a 'gigolo' who preyed
on lonely older women. That's probably true of
the man whom you claim has been following
you. What on earth were you doing in Feminine
Hygiene?

Anyway, dear, the photo is to remind you of
happier times and, whatever our ups and
downs, how fond I am of you.

Good luck on your travels,

Vera

Dear Vera,

Your letter arrived just as I was leaving The Limes, so am replying en route to Australia and what will undoubtedly be the grateful and heart-felt embrace of my daughter Lesley. She's so self-less – even at nearly eight-and-half-months 'enceinte', she tried every reason she could think of to put me off coming to help her. Although she did, of course, buy me my plane ticket.

Thank you for the photograph, and what I take to be your apology in not quite so many words. Up here, speeding through the cerebral blue sky, sipping my second complimentary Bloody Mary and chewing my nuts, I already feel calmer and less frazzled than I have felt in donkey's ages, even though I hate heights.

I remember the gigolo incident very well – better, evidently, than you. It was indeed on Capri. You claimed you had 'forgotten' to take your spectacles out with you – although I knew of course it was only vanity – so did not see the hourly rates written on the back of what you cared to think of as the gentleman in question's calling card. You were giggling and fluttering at him and were about to be dragged off to an hotel room arm-in-arm with the odious creature, when I took the card myself and warned you of the expense you were about to incur – a hundred thousand lire for half an hour! Even then, as I remember, you asked him if he took traveller's cheques.

The man who followed me was of an entirely different caste. His hair was unBrillianteened, for starters. He was about forty or so, with natural wavy hair, rather like the colour mine used to be before I went grey – a kind of spun gold with amber threads. He was tall, handsome and quite distinguished looking. However, not being as easy prey as you (and, lest we forget, this was the man who allegedly ransacked my rubbish bin for purposes unknown), I went into the Feminine Hygiene aisle of the supermarket to shake him off, which I did – haven't you ever noticed it's a no-go area for men? Clive was just the same when he was alive. As far as he cared to be aware, I never had a single period in thirty-five years of marriage. Don't know why I'm going into this – must be the Bloody Marys.

All for now, as my in-flight supper is about to be served – I've opted for the boeuf bourguignon, but peering over at the opposite aisle, it looks like common-or-garden stew from here. Will post this from Melbourne when I get there (the letter, not the meal!). I think Lesley now has a home computer, so will send you an e-mail address soon for speedier correspondence.

Fond regards,

Irene

Dear Irene,

Ma tells me you suddenly took off for Oz, so I'll send this to Lesley's. I'm so glad you've made it up with her – Lesley's a great girl and well worth the price of the airfare.

I've enclosed a good-luck card and note for her, as it's ages since we were in touch. Be sure and let us have your e-mail address, asap.

Can't speak for Ma, but love from the rest of us,

Karen

Dear Lesley,

How are you, me old matey? Ready to pop?
Bet you can't wait to get rid of it. To think in a
couple of months I'll have three kids! More fool
me for believing St John when he said I
couldn't get pregnant while I was breast-
feeding. You'd think a medical man would know,
but being a vet, he's obviously more familiar
with a cow's insides than a woman's. Actually,
I'm sure he misled me on purpose. He's got
some loopy idea about breeding a rugby team.
It's all those bloody litters he delivers. Well, he
can dream on. I'm definitely having my tubes
tied after this one. Ma's on his side, naturally.
She thinks the sun shines out of his arse.
Talking of which, she won't get any grandchildren from my brother Howard and his partner
Antony, though having said that, I believe
they're thinking of surrogacy. Hope they're not
expecting me to offer!

It must be a nightmare Irene arriving out of
the blue. It's St John's fault for telling her about
lastminute.com. She descended on us just when
we'd managed to pack Ma off on holiday. I had
to retreat to The Bothy's turret to get a bit of
privacy.

Ma, like the poor, is always with us. She's
gone quite batty and is currently insisting she's

being 'stalked' round Little Shagthorne by a 'handsome younger man'. If only. Most of the blokes round here look like serial killers.

I really miss our good times together. We were a pair of naughty Sheilas, weren't we? None of that in the dull old Dales! I *have* got a couple of cannabis plants in the greenhouse. Ma keeps asking when they're going to grow tomatoes.

Good luck with the birth. I'm wincing and crossing my legs at the thought of it.

Wish I was there to crack a slab of tinnies with you.

Loads of love,

Karen

PS How's Brian shaping up? Have you managed to stop him wearing the tight tee-shirts?

PPS My e-mail address for more 'personal' correspondence! karen@greatshag.com

Dear Irene,

I hope you're settled in and over your jet-lag, which must have been considerable if you drank Bloody Marys all the way. I can imagine what a killer feeling lonely and unwanted can be, but you're not falling back into your old habits, are you?

I expect your family are pleased to have you. Well, your granddaughter Cheryl Marie anyway. They're always insecure with a new brother or sister on the way. Sabrina still hasn't got over Nelson's arrival and now she's got another one coming. I can't help but feel Karen is very selfish.

She's gone quite batty, it must be the hormones. Keeps insisting she needs more 'space'. Goodness knows why in a house with twelve bedrooms! She's taken to spending most of the time in the West Wing's 'turret', now re-christened 'Karen's Kave'. There's a retractable ladder and bolts on the door. I don't know what she's doing up there, but I hope she's growing her hair. At this rate St John will only be able to exercise his 'rights' if he climbs up it.

I was rather alarmed at your description of the man you say was following you. It exactly fits one I keep encountering here. He was staring at me in the butcher's the other day. I'd gone in for a pound of shank, but I bought four pig's trotters, it was so unnerving. I mentioned it to Karen, when she clambered down for lunch, but her only response was to complain about a toe-nail in the curry. Were there any letters with my address, torn up in your dustbin? The odd thing is, he looks vaguely familiar – especially the hair – but I just can't place him.

Time to put Rex on his lead and Nelson in his pram and collect Sabrina from school. St John's put the Land Rover at my disposal, but it keeps me fit trotting up and down the hills. I expect *you'll* soon be run off your feet!

Warm regards to you all,

Vera

St Urban
Melbourne
Australia
e-mail: irene@ozmail.com

Dear Vera,

Arrived here in one piece but without luggage, which apparently has been lost somewhere in Koala Lumpur, wherever that is. What is it about Australia, me, and clothes? Last time I was here, as you may remember, Lesley sent all my luggage back to England and I was forced to improvise with your old cast-offs. This time I am wearing Lesley's pre-maternity wardrobe, which she rather crossly warned me she wants back next week. On Wednesday, to be precise. Apparently she has booked herself in for a Caesarian section next Tuesday at 11.00 am, as she doesn't want the inconvenience of not knowing when she might go into labour. Can you imagine? Talk about the Want-It-Now-Got-To-Have-It-Spoilt-Baby-Generation! I wouldn't mind, but she kept me waiting weeks before she would deign to pop out of me – by Dr Crank's calculations I was eleven-and-a-half months pregnant before he clamped her little head between his forceps.

Little Cheryl Marie, of course, is delighted to have her old Granny Spencer back again. My, how she's grown! We've just been having a rather difficult conversation about how babies

55

get into mummies' tummies. I bit the bullet and told her the truth about daddies putting their wee-wees into mummies' front bottoms, but I'm afraid she thought it rather implausible. Can't say I blame her.

Lesley is screaming in the kitchen for some reason at the moment, so it's hard to concentrate. Will 'send' this now. Isn't e-mail magic?

Love,

Irene

PS Don't know why you think my Mystery Man would be following you, and he certainly couldn't have got your address from my dustbin. As you know, I value order, organisation, and neatness above everything, so I file your letters in a folder called 'Correspondence', where I interleave them with the rough copies of my missives to you. However much they might irritate me at times, I would never tear them up and 'bin' them.

PPS I will not dignify your comments about 'drinking' and 'old habits' with a reply. Suffice it to say that some people might say that three Bloody Marys, a bottle of wine and a couple of brandies consumed within a stressful twenty-four-hour period, which was spent willing my plane to stay in the sky, was on the light side and only common sense.

Dear Irene

Sorry to have been tardy in my response, but we have had high dramas at Little Shagthorne. I knew Karen was playing fast and loose with fate, as well as St John, with her blasted ladder, and sure enough last Friday, blimp-sized as she is, she slipped and tumbled down it. In seconds she was groaning and thrashing around with contractions, two months early! As this 'Gimme, Gimme, Gimme' generation find out, God works in mysterious ways, particularly with labour. She's now in Gt Shagthorne Cottage Hospital maternity ward, with her feet higher than her head, a position with which, I'm afraid, she is all too familiar. She'll have to hold it for longer than usual, though. The hospital won't allow a premature birth, they haven't got the incubators.

I must say, it's been lovely for us all to have the peace. The children have been much happier and even St John is far from inconsolable. He, poor boy, has to do the round trip to the hospital after his veterinarian surgery every day, to fulfil Karen's demands for delicatessen food and foot rubs. Fortunately, there's always one of my delicious dishes on the table when he gets home. He often eats it and passes out, absolutely exhausted.

Sheepdipper's has had its events, too. I don't know whether I mentioned it, but Howard and Antony have been trying for a surrogate baby. I suppose they got the idea from the sheep flock's artificial insemination. An agency has put them in touch with a young woman who's willing to help. Quite who supplies the wiggly bits, and how they get into her, I haven't liked to ask. Something to do with saucers. If you think 'wee wees and front bottoms' are tricky, try explaining that one to a seven-year-old!

The whole story is going to be documented by Dales TV, our local cable channel. Howard and Antony are delighted – they see 'A Life With Sheep', as Dales TV are calling it, as good publicity for their yoghurt. The TV company hasn't got a lot of money for the production – apparently their Internet launch was a disaster – so another bonus is that they have accepted my offer to do the 'location' catering. It'll be an excellent opportunity to expand my repertoire. Did I tell you I've got publishers begging for a proposal?

With all the excitement, I nearly forgot your 'Mystery Man'. But he, it seems, hasn't forgotten me. Yesterday he popped up again, pointing and gesticulating outside the delicatessen. I'd gone in to get Karen some creme frâiche, but she ended up with chopped liver. It is disturbing. He's obviously trying to communicate something, unless, of course, he just has a nervous affliction.

Well, dear, I must get on. A Grandma's work is never done, as I am sure you have re-discovered.

Good Luck to Lesley – her baby must be due any moment? And to you,

Vera

Dear Vera,

Found out why Lesley was screaming – she was giving birth to a baby girl on kitchen floor! Can't stop. More tomorrow.

Irene

Dear Vera,

Well, talk about the best laid plans of mice and pregnant women . . . ! After all the trouble she went to, booking the best doctors and anaesthetist and a private room, and thinking she can just play God and 'decide' to have her baby delivered on an operating table at a time that's convenient to her busy little diary, my daughter Lesley gave birth to her new baby girl on the kitchen floor braced between the washing machine and the tumble dryer, while I was e-mailing you. By the time I got to her it was practically all over – I just had to clean up and cut the cord with the kitchen scissors. The paramedics said I'd done a very professional job, but then I've seen it performed so many times on 'Peak Practice'. The baby is beautiful and has the most luxurious strawberry-blonde curly hair, so although they're going to christen her Sarah Jane, we call her Bubbles. Given that her mother was watching her laundry go through on the woollen setting when she was arriving, it seems appropriate all round! Unfortunately I was so busy with Lesley's nether regions, I didn't have time to notice my other little granddaughter, Cheryl Marie, watching intently from the doorway. After witnessing the mysteries of birth at close quarters

61

she is now inclined to believe my story about how babies are made, and has started glaring angrily at Brian, Lesley's partner, every time he comes in the house. Mind you, I'm afraid I do likewise. His divorce isn't through yet so my poor little Bubbles is illegitimate. What times we live in. I'm afraid the concept of 'family' that we grew up with has just sailed down the Swanee.

Have had time now to read your last e-mail properly, and am so sorry to hear about your poor daughter Karen's troubles. Is she still managing to keep the baby inside her? But then again, why wouldn't the little mite be in a hurry to get out, when its parents were in such a rush to get it in, so to speak? Everything is 'Now' with this generation – they've no concept of planning and waiting and patience.

Got to go. Lesley's shouting for a cup of tea, and I'd better check Bubbles' nappy.

With much love, from one exhausted Granny to another!

Irene

PS If you do go ahead with selling your recipes, ask your publishers if they would like a proposal for an Australian cookery book. I've found a wonderful way with fricasseed emu.

Dear Irene,

Congratulations! Another little girl. I do so hope my daughter Karen doesn't have another boy. Nelson's not walking yet, though goodness knows his legs are long enough, and he's already such a handful. When I asked Sabrina what she'd like her mummy to have next, she said 'a supply of condoms'. Perhaps she understands more about the process than I thought. I'll never know the half of the things she learned when we lived on that trailer park.

Anyway, whatever sex Karen's baby is, it's still inside. Unlike my son Howard and his partner Antony's. They've had a terrible time trying to get their 'host' mother, Natasha, pregnant. Turns out they've both got low sperm count. Has there been a case of that on 'Peak Practice'? Howard blames Antony for riding horses in his youth. Antony blames Howard for wearing tight trousers. They both blame each other for eating too much fish. Apparently the salmon round here are riddled with female hormones. They've had the most awful rows about it and all in front of the Dales TV cameras! I never realised how 'intimate' 'A Life With Sheep' would be. It's years since I've seen Howard's private parts and now he's sharing them with the nation. Thank goodness they've enlisted the help of St John and his veterinarian syringe. I just pray Dales TV put a bag over Natasha's head before they film what he does with it.

The good news is my 'location' catering has been a great success. The director says he's never known a film crew get back to work so fast! I've almost run out of Indian recipes – they seem to have meal breaks every half an hour – so if you'd like to send me your fricassee one, I'll give it a go. There's an ostrich farm near Sheepdipper's, so I can substitute that for emu.

Lots of love to you all and a big kiss for 'Bubbles'. With a name like that, she'll certainly be carrying on the family traditions. Have one for me,

Vera

Dear Vera,

It is amazing, the speed of this e-mail business, isn't it? One of the products of this 'Now' generation that I approve of. And talk about the saving on postage! I'm thinking that I might buy a computer myself when I get back to Hethergreen so I can continue to communicate electronically. I couldn't sleep last night, so I started 'scurfing the web' as I've seen your little Sabrina do, and you'd be 'gobsmacked' (to use Lesley's favourite word) to know what you can do on it. You can go anywhere and buy anything. You'd never need to leave your house again if you didn't want to. Must be a boon to agoraphobics.

Back to your last missive, I do think you're being over-critical of Baby Boy Nelson – how on earth could he be expected to be walking at his age? I wonder if you're not being tainted with this 'Now' business yourself? As for Howard, I don't wonder you sound shocked about his goings on. For myself, I can't say in all honesty that I want you to continue to keep me informed about his and Antony's progress in that department. Personally I was happier in the old days when Section 28 went unchallenged.

I think there's been a misunderstanding about my Australian recipes. I didn't mean for *you* to have them. I just thought that your publisher might be interested in *me* doing my *own* book. And frankly, if you're going to muck about changing vital ingredients it defeats the object – an Australian recipe book should be full of Australian produce, not what's currently available in Great Shagthorne.

Thank you, incidentally, for sending a kiss to Bubbles. I shall gloss over your illusion to 'family traditions' about drinking. I've been skimming through some of Lesley's psychology self-help books. Have you ever heard of 'projection'? I'll leave it with you to think about.

Must trot off. I've rejoined the Creative Writing for Senior Citizens class now I'm back in Melbourne, and it's my first session today.

With fondest regards,

Irene

Dear Irene,

I don't know that I do approve of this addiction to speed. E-mail is all very well, but it's put me in touch with so many foreign parts and each one expects an answer, not so much 'Now' as 'Yesterday'. It's sometimes two in the morning when I lay down my weary head, having satisfied my global correspondents.

There isn't a 'shoot' today, they're still waiting for the results from the last insemination (don't know how the 'mother' bore up, but St John got back knackered) so, for once, I've got time to myself. I decided to indulge in some much needed peace and reflection and, as you see, I'm writing this in the greenhouse. It's so pleasant to be surrounded by growing things. I'm sitting next to Karen's tomato plants, which I, of course, have been left to tend. They are a beautiful shade of viridian and I'm breathing in their earthy scent, which I must say is very lulling . . .

Whoops, dropped off there for a while. Now if I'd been at the computer, I'd have crashed onto the keyboard, deleted everything and got an imprint of the alphabet on my forehead. See what I mean? Going at my own pace, slow and steady, I'll achieve much more. You might want to consider that point, if your psycho-self-help books haven't already made it . . .

Oh dear, dozed off again. Really, the atmosphere in here is very 'heady' . . . I feel like I've had a glass too many. Following in your footsteps! Talking of footsteps, I think I'd better have a little walk. I'll leave Nelson . . . even he's less hyperactive than usual . . . snoozing in his pram, as the ground outside's very bumpy. Karen ordered the garden to be landscaped as part of The Bothy renovations, but like the rest of her plans, it's on 'hold'.

Much later:

In bed, with slight concussion. Can't read the above, owing to double vision, but I think I mentioned the garden's in upheaval. In fact, to call it a demolition site wouldn't be exaggerating. I was a little wobbly on my feet, no doubt due to the unaccustomed cat-nap, and I hadn't taken three steps before I'd tumbled into the pit which is destined to become the kidney-shaped swimming pool. No workmen around of course, all on their 'lunch-break' at 3.30. Really, they're worse than the film crew! I lay there stunned, with black specks circling (turns out there actually were some crows, or as Karen would have it when St John told her, vultures, overhead).

Then, Irene, the strangest thing! Against the

sunlight I saw this dark, towering silhouette. Naturally, in my concussed state, I thought I was in an episode of 'The X-Files' and was about to be abducted by extra-terrestrials. But he, for it was a 'He', dragged me up the bank and carried me to the shelter of The Coach House. He seemed to know exactly where I lived, sat me on the sofa, made me a cup of tea and at last I got a proper look at him. Guess who he was? None other than your 'Mystery Man'!

Unfortunately, I passed out at that point and when I came round, St John was bending over me with a bucket of water. 'He' had disappeared without trace. When I tried to explain it to St John, he put a cold flannel on my head and told me to stop 'babbling'.

This must be more than coincidence. Who on earth – or out of it – is he?

Yours, in awe,

Vera

Dear Vera,

Call Hethergreen police immediately and ask for DC Hogg. Tell him about 'The Stalker' moving to Shagthorne. And tell him from me I have no intention of returning to England until he is in police custody (Stalker, not Hogg). And in the meantime, don't go out yourself. If you do have to nip down to the shops or something, keep a very tight hold on your handbag. Young men only follow old women for one thing. I mean, look – you were concussed – how do you know for sure and certain that you *tripped* into the pool? Couldn't you have been pushed? And now he's been inside your house he'll no doubt be back, having 'cased the joint' while you were unconscious.

I showed your e-mail to Lesley, who thinks I'm over-reacting and has been trying to talk me out of getting you to tell the police. She sends her best wishes for your speedy recovery, however, and asks if you or St John could take Karen's 'laptop' to her in the hospital, as she is sending her an e-mail. She is most insistent about it, but then they did get on like a house on fire when they were here together last year.

Look after yourself, dear, and take things easy. Leave the film crew to fend for themselves until you're fully recovered – they'd probably welcome fish and chips anyway after all your 'exotica'.

Much love and all good wishes for a brief but thorough convalescence,

Irene

Dear Karen,

Your Mum got stoned in your greenhouse just from the atmosphere of what she calls 'the tomatoes', and then claims to have seen a stalker – must be good stuff! But my Mum's mailed her to call in the cops, so you'd better get St John to move the plants or harvest them quick.

Brian has turned out to be really boring. He was much more interesting when he had a wife to go home to. Mum's going on about marriage, but I'm thinking of telling him to bog off.

Better go – she keeps sneaking in and trying to read this over my shoulder. Isn't it hell having the old bags staying with us?

Love,

Lesley

Dear Irene,

Took your advice and rang DC Hogg but all I got was his 'voice mail'. He hasn't returned my call yet. Obviously Hethergreen is a hotbed of crime and he's out stopping it. You don't have his e-mail address do you?

I've stayed indoors since the incident. I even considered moving up into Karen's turret, but decided I was in danger of becoming angora-phobic. Besides, Mystery Man seemed far from menacing. He had a lovely smile . . . almost angelic. I wish I could place whom he reminds me of . . . Someone's banging wildly on my front door. Whoever can that be at 1.45 in the morning? I'll just get St John's animal tranquil-liser darts . . .

2.00 am

False alarm. It was Howard in tears, after another tiff with Antony. Dales TV has suspended filming. They say it's lost the 'feel-good' factor. Judging from what they've put on the screen so far, I suspect they mean literally.

Must finish and bring Howard round. I shot off the tranquilliser dart before I realised it was only him.

More soon,

Vera

Dearest Lesley,

No worries. Sent St John to sort the Old Bill at our local Masonic. Deal is they get three plants and we get two. I've got them here in my hospital room, hidden behind the pots of bloody crysanths your Ma sent me. Not that I can reach them with my legs in bloody stirrups. Put me off bondage for ever! Like you, fed up with bloody men, bloody babies and bloody mothers.

Bloody love,

Karen

Dear Vera,

I don't know DC Hogg's e-mail address –
when I was dealing with him I was still
'computer illiterate' – but for heaven's sake,
keep trying to get him on the phone. I can't
imagine why he hasn't been available –
Hethergreen is, for the most part, a peaceful
village. Normally the only time the police are
at full stretch is when they do crowd control at
the annual historic event of 'Kicking The Pig's
Bladder'. Obviously you can't stay indoors for
ever, but neither can you live in constant terror
of being thrown into empty swimming pools by
a Perpetrator Unknown. Using your son-in-law
St John's veterinarian tranquilliser gun to
defend yourself was an inspiration, but if you
go round firing it off by mistake like that, the
whole of Shagthorne, both Little and Great,
will be asleep. How is your poor son Howard
now?

It is the weekend here in Australia. I suppose
it is in England too, but once again I feel so
far away (which I am) that I find it hard to
imagine it still exists. Thank heavens for the
e-mail – such a lifeline.

My daughter Lesley and her partner Brian
have gone away for a couple of days, leaving
me with the usual expressed breast milk in the

fridge, and in sole charge of my two grand-daughters. Lesley and Brian have been having 'problems', apparently, and need to be alone to remind themselves quite what they saw in each other in the first place. Honestly! If they can't remember after this short time, what on earth are their memories going to be like when they get to our age? And how terrible to break up Brian's marriage and *then* wonder if they've done the right thing. But that's typical of Lesley. She's always been faddy. She never enjoyed any of her Christmas presents when she was little, because by the time she'd posted her letter to Santa up the chimney and we'd retrieved it and bought it all accordingly, she'd gone off everything on the list. Sometimes I wonder if our generation wasn't so elated that the war was over, and so determined that our children should inherit a brave new world with free this and free that, all we succeeded in doing was to spoil them and give them unreasonable expectations of life. I mean, what would Winston Churchill make of things if he were still with us? He must be rolling in his grave.

Baby Bubbles is crying for her 4.00 am feed, so I must stop. I'm exhausted but can't seem to sleep. Too much worry. The good news, though, is that the airline have finally found my luggage – it wasn't in Koala Lumpur, but Helsinki! – so at least I now recognise myself when I look in the mirror. I looked a real sight in Lesley's crop tops.

Reply soon, old friend. I'm so lonely.

Love,

Irene

Dear Irene,

Your e-mail made my heart bleed. Oh, I do so
know what you mean about being lonely.
Sometimes it's at its worst when you're in the
bosom of your family. I said as much straight to
camera, on Dales TV's 'A Life With Sheep'
yesterday. The camera crew were almost in
tears. Howard was furious with me. I'd come
out for a visit (I'd love to see Oz after all your
tales, though St Urban doesn't sound quite as
exotic as India), but I'm absolutely indispens-
able here. My daughter Karen's in hospital for
the foreseeable future – she made so much fuss
about 'privacy' they've moved her to her own
room, for which, of course, St John is paying.
He, poor lamb, is rushed off his feet with two
veterinarian surgeries a day and all the
'outreach' visits. He's had to go back several
times to see my son Howard and his partner
Antony's surrogate mother – trouble with the
syringe, or something – but the good news is,
they are, at last, pregnant! Howard is over the
moon. Now he and Antony are arguing about
which of their little squiggles did it!

As they've 'got a result' (TV parlance) and
everyone's smiling again, Dales TV are back.
The director, a nice lad despite his stubble, said
I was wasted behind the scenes, and I should

get in front of the camera. I took to it like a natural. I don't know that I've ever confided to you that when I was a girl I longed to tread the boards. Over the years many people have told me that with my vibrant personality and flair for music and dance, I should have. Of course my father would never have tolerated it. To him an actress was no different to a prostitute. It was only because his local pub was called the Nell Gwynne and was a notorious haunt of 'ladies of the night'. I often wondered, if he felt so strongly about them, why he went there.

Now, Irene, I'm saying this for your own good. DO NOT GO BACK TO THE BOTTLE. No matter how desperate you feel, resist it old friend, or it's not only Winston Churchill who'll be rolling around in his grave. I know he's one of your heroes, but there are some of his footsteps in which you wouldn't want to follow.

Needless to say, I mean the above in a loving, caring, way.

Your own,

Vera

Dear Lesley,

What's happening with boring Brian? Have you made it up or kicked him out?

Things have improved in here since I got the private room. I'm allowed to move about, as long as I don't leave the hospital. As if? I can't bear the idea of going back to The Bothy. It's too full of St John and the bloody kids. Seriously thinking of running away, as soon as I've dumped this one. They'd be much happier with Ma looking after them. Thank God she *is* there, leaving me to put my feet up (literally) and smoke a spliff! Course she loves it, keeps going on about being 'needed'. Hope I'm dead before I have to justify being alive like our mothers do.

Run out of magazines, so I've been surfing the Net looking at porn sites. We could do much better, you know! Send us a mail soon, I'm so bored.

Karen

Dear Vera,

You may down-cry Sir Winston all you like,
but just ask yourself in a quiet moment what he
would have said about your son-in-law St John
– who, lest we forget, is a *vet*, not a gynaecolo-
gist – impregnating a paid stranger on television
with a syringe full of semen from two homosex-
uals, one of which is your *own son,* so that she
may bring forth this strange fruit and hand it
over for cash to said deviants to bring up.
Personally I would fight them on the beaches
every time. Instead, you encourage it! And you
say that the 'good news' is that they've
succeeded! Call me old-fashioned if you will,
but who can the little mite call 'Mother' when
it's born?

Meanwhile, here in Melbourne, I am having
to cope with a new granddaughter born out of
wedlock because my daughter Lesley couldn't
keep her hands off another woman's husband.
It's certainly not what I, or indeed my late
husband Clive, ever thought we were fighting
the Gerries for. We might just as well have
handed over our green and pleasant land to
Adolf if that's what we'd wanted. I'm just left
feeling that the more time goes by, the more of
my life seems to have been in vain.

However, 'nil desperado, Irene' has always

81

been my battlecry, and to this end I managed to have a good long chat with Brian, Lesley's partner, the other evening, on our own while Lesley was resting. (Though goodness knows what she's got to be tired about – I seem to be the only one to notice when little Bubbles needs feeding or changing.) But back to my main thrust . . . I managed finally after some subtle hyperbowl (thank heavens for my Creative Writing Course!) to fire Brian up enough to promise to push through his divorce with all his vim and vigour to a speedy conclusion. Apparently the papers are just sitting on his solicitor's desk, so I don't know what's been keeping him. I made him hold little Bubbles in his arms and swear on her dear little golden head that he would make her legitimate, albeit retrospectfully. He seemed quite enthusiastic by the end, and called me Mother, and thanked me. He's been out and bought Lesley a socking great engagement ring at vast expense, which he showed me today in secret, with tears in his eyes, and he's going to propose officially at the weekend. *This*, Vera, is what *I* think of as the role of the responsible mother, whatever her age – guiding her children towards a more wholesome lifestyle, not giddily encouraging them to go their own way as you do with yours. For instance, if a son of mine had told me he was 'gay' in his confused early years, I would have explained to him that it was just a whim, and not something that had to be acted upon. I would have reminded him of those old-fashioned notions 'will power' and 'self denial'. I would have introduced him to every eligible girl within a fifty-mile radius of Great Shagthorne, and if they had failed to raise a response, I would have told him to just keep his hand on his ha'penny. One thing I would definitely *not* have done would be to egg him on about artificial insemination. But that is obviously where we differ.

Once more I shall gloss over your illusions to my so-called drinking habit. Honestly, talk about the pot calling the kettle! *You* may have chosen to forget who it was who had seventeen 'Long Slow Screws' in Majorca when we were on our tour of Europe, but I certainly haven't. Nor have I forgotten the consequences, but I shall not go down that alley just now. I shall merely say 'Manolo' and leave you to weave your way unsteadily down Memory Lane. But besides, here in Australia, where it is extremely hot, it would be folly not to constantly replace precious lost body fluids on a regular basis with a few glasses of wine or a couple of lagers. Quite apart from a little liquid libation helping my hypertension in this stressful environment that I find myself living in.

I feel absolutely drained after writing such a long missive, but as your friend it had to be done. Naturally it goes without saying that I, too, mean everything aforementioned in the most loving and caring way. But of course a lot of your behaviour clicks into place now I know your father frequented a bawdy house. Nobody would argue that it was a nice beginning for you, Vera, but if you're determined to try, you can rise above the nasty bits in your gene pool.

With all loving and friendly wishes,

Irene

Dear Irene,

You know where you can stuff your 'loving and friendly wishes'!

Vera

Dear Lesley,

I hear you're going to marry boring Brian after all. Ma showed me a rambling e-mail Irene had sent her when she'd obviously had a few 'tinnies' too many. We noticed she was back on the sauce when she was here. Perhaps it was a mistake to let her share a room with the home-brewing kit. I wouldn't leave her alone with the kids if I were you. Unless, of course, you want to come back to find she's fallen into the chip-pan and set the house on fire. Ha, ha, only joking! Anyway, girl, she reckons Brian's bought you a 'socking great engagement ring' so don't go giving him back to his wife 'til you've got it safely on your finger. I haven't got a wedding ring on mine any more. My finger had puffed up like a black pudding and the triage nurse had to saw it off (ring not finger). Think it's an omen?

Brett (the triage nurse) is a mate of Howard and Antony's and a real pet. Pops in to share a spliff and has promised to sneak me some phar-maceutical Charlie. St John won't give me class As and has even tried to get me off the weed while I'm sprogging. Sanctimonious bastard. He's lolloping down the ward now, with a pound of healthy bananas. Urgh!

Karen

Dear Irene,

My mother showed me your last e-mail, which had us all in tears. Antony and I were shocked to the fundament at your medieval attitudes – haven't you ever watched the TV drama 'Queer As Folk'? Not that Great Shagthorne is exactly a gay village, more's the pity. Your comments were especially hurtful after the way we've always welcomed you here. Last time, if I remember rightly, you said we were gorgeous boys and you wished we were *your* sons. You even encouraged us to try for adoption, saying why not, we were 'just like a married couple'? Of course, by then you had had the greater part of two bottles of Sheepdipper's Chardonnay. We can only conclude you've joined that band of losers darling Tony Blair calls 'the forces of conservatism' who read the *Sun*, go fox hunting and are deeply homophobic. Fortunately, with this government, they are in a minority.

Age is no excuse for embracing the attitudes of Hitler, even if the last war is still your yardstick. Mother may have other foibles, but she is remarkably open and tolerant about sex. Things she told us about your travels together, which at the time we were inclined to disbelieve, now make perfect sense. The only 'Manolo' she remembers, by the way, was a bartender over whom you threw a jug of sangria. She was particularly annoyed, as it was before she'd had a glass of it.

I daresay you will find excuses for all of this, but they will fall on deaf ears at Sheepdipper's. It's such a pity, as we were going to invite you to be Godmother to our baby when he/she is born. But now we're going to get a lesbian friend from Stonewall. We don't want our child growing up with weird ideas about what makes a proper family.

Yours,

Howard

Dear Vera and Howard

Got your e-mails and am in a torment of retribution. I read mine again. Think I went over the top. Please forget and forgive. Don't know what got into me. If I had a hair shirt, I'd be wearing it.

Sometimes I wonder if I'm not a little bit depressed.

Yours penitentuarily,

Irene

Dear Vera and Howard,

I have been in a torment of agony since I e-mailed my apology to you both a few days ago, having heard nothing in return. Did you get the flowers I sent yet, Howard? And Vera, have you received the cookery book I found for you, 'A Hundred-and-One Ways to Serve Kangaroo Imaginatively'? I'm not fishing for gratitude, merely checking.

As always, I have found some solace in the Creative Arts, and send you this poem, which woke me up in the middle of the night demanding to be penned. I hope and pray that it may go some way to stop me being a 'persona non gratis' in your eyes.

I really do value our friendship, and hope and pray that it does not continue to be 'erstwhile'.

With a heart filled with shame,

Irene

An Ode

by
Irene Spencer

They say that all the world's a stage,
And we mere players on it,
So your humbled servant, I Irene,
Give you this modest sonnet,
To make amends, to build a bridge,
To mend what I did ravage,
I never meant to you offend,
Let alone be savage.

You looked to me for friendship,
As indeed you should,
But all I gave you in return
Was to drag you through the mud.
I wish that I could turn back time,
And have never ever sent
The e-mail, writ impulsively,
In which my rage was spent.

Dear Vera Small, and Howard too,
(That sweet fruit of your loins)
If apologies were money
I would shower you both with coins.
Please look at me with love again,
And don't be filled with hate,
Excuses are empty as I know,
But I've not been too well of late.

The Coach House Apartment
The Bothy
Little Shagthorne
vera'svoyages@littleshag.com

Dear Irene,

I have pondered long and hard on whether to accept your apology, albeit put off by the appalling doggerel. I do hope you're not throwing good money away on this 'creative writing course'. I was in such a quandary about it, I even e-mailed my global network for advice. It seems to have struck a chord, I 'downloaded' lots of replies. Obviously a plethora of people feel abused by their so-called friends. My Indian pals Raj and Shiva (boys@bumchums.com) think I should definitely forgive you. They say it will bring me 'good Karma'. But there again every beggar in India will promise you that for twenty rupees. Our old acquaintance Ethel Roscoe (ethel@homelyfaggot.co.uk) feels this time you've gone too far and I should on no account forgive and forget. Did I mention she bought a PC at a boot fair and found it was still loaded with the personal details of her bank manager? It's been awfully useful in her application for a loan – though perhaps not so good for her Karma. Yasmin – remember Yasmin, my next door neighbour on the trailer park?

(psychic@farshores.com) – gave you an absent Tarot reading and came up with the Queen of Cups – she's the one holding a large wine glass and surrounded by flagons. She says to leave that with you. Even silly old Edward Blunt, your erstwhile suitor (blunt@fowlshag.com), stuck in his oar, or should I say straw! He says you've kept your hand on your own ha'penny for so long (I've no idea how he knows) you haven't noticed there's been devaluation.

After many sleepless nights (answering the dratted e-mail!) I've finally decided to excuse your behaviour. It is, as our long history demonstrates, ingrained in my nature. Besides, I know the sort of things you get up to when you're 'depressed' and I couldn't bear to have that on my conscience. I blame a lot on your 'creative writing'.

My son Howard and his partner Antony say thank you for the bouquet of birds of paradise. They're an outlandish sight in Great Shagthorne, but I daresay they are common or garden, perhaps literally, in Australia. Anyway, they have pride of place by the four-poster bed in a heritage-style milking bucket, and the boys say to tell you they had a lot of fun with the spiky bits.

I'm enclosing a booklet my granddaughter Sabrina brought home from school on sex education (which reminds me, 'A Hundred-and-One Ways With a Kangaroo' went straight in the bin). If this explanatory little work persuades playground bullies to behave like fully functioning citizens (which I doubt – Sabrina is called all sorts of names because she has short hair and likes football), it may have the same effect on you. At least it will provide an alternative to your blind, clishay-ridden prejudices.

All for now. Must stop and do something important, like work on my recipe book proposal. My stints as a 'performer' on 'A Life With Sheep' have made me wonder about a TV cookery programme to accompany the book. Of course I'd have to include more local dishes, like scrag-end and toad in the hole. I mentioned the idea to our director and he said he'd pass it on, with some comments about my catering.

I advise *you* to do something practical next time you feel a poem coming on.

Vera

Dear Vera,

Thank you for your e-mail at last – I can't tell you how relieved I am that we're speaking again. And thank you for the very informative booklet on sex education. I learnt more perusing that for half an hour than I have hitherto learnt in a lifetime. I'm rather cross with Edward Blunt, though, for being so indiscrete on my behalf. And, as always, there are two sides to that story. All *I* was after was friendship, but it appears he had other things on his mind, which I kept trying to ignore. You remember finding his truss in your apartment after I'd been staying there? I'd just popped out to make some tea, and when I returned to the living room, he was in his birthday suit, lolling on the chaise longue! I was so shocked I dropped his cup in his lap, hence (after a lot of agonised hopping about and blue language) his hasty departure and forgetfulness in the underwear department.

I'm not normally prone to depression, as you know, except when I'm in Australia. It seems I travel all those thousands of miles each time just to be ignored by my daughter and treated like a maid-of-all-work. Of course it's wonderful to see my grandchildren, just not every minute of every day. I feel anxious all the time here,

95

and get funny thoughts that keep me awake half the night. Like about being upside down. Just think of the globe – there you are in England, standing the right way up, your head in the air, and here I am with my head dangling down into space. It can't be good for me, can it? Apart from the blood rushing to my head as a consequence, I get the most awful cramp in my feet, which is a result of clinging on frantically with my toes so I don't fall off into the void. I wonder that all Australians are not constantly at the chiropodist. But I suppose they've been brought up to know no better.

I have been worrying too about the Mystery Man Stalker that I left behind me in Blighty. My next-door neighbour Beryl wrote to me last week, telling me she'd seen him again hanging around my house. Did you ever get to speak to DC Hogg of Hethergreen CID? Do please try again if you haven't. You may unwittingly be holding vital information that a thorough interrogation by a police officer might uncover through their skilful questioning techniques.

Please give my love to Howard and Antony, and say I'm glad they liked the flowers. You don't mention if you tried making any of the dishes before you 'binned' the kangaroo book (heavens, you *must* have been cross with me – I've never known you look a gift horse in the mouth before). I had thought you might like to adapt some of the recipes for lamb and mutton from the boys' farm.

Baby Bubbles is crying to be changed and it's almost time to collect Cheryl Marie from school, so I'll have to finish.

Yours in haste and heartfelt gratitude,

Irene xx

Dear Irene,

I'd been wondering what had happened to the
Mystery Man, I haven't seen him at all since
the swimming pool incident. In fact, I've rather
missed him. I felt we'd established a 'bond'. I
tried DC Hogg again, but although I left
another message, he didn't return my call (no
wonder the police are always calling for extra
resources), so I dropped the enclosed note to
him. Hope that will be of some use.

I'm so glad you discovered the truth about
Edward Blunt before you got too involved. I
didn't like to say so before, but I had a similar
problem with him. We'd been to a Countryside
Alliance rally where Edward was making a
speech in support of fox hunting (he is, when
all's said and done, a poultry farmer). Edward
got carried away with all the cheering and back-
slapping and waving of the St George's flag
and, when taking me home, threw me on my
back in the poultry van and attempted to have
his way with me.

Fortunately, he'd had one too many Old
Peculiars and I was able to fend him off quite
easily. I shoved a knee in his crutch (hence the
truss) and crowned him with a chicken basket.
While he was rolling around in fowl droppings,
I gave him a piece of my mind – and whatever

he said, that's *all* I gave him. I'm afraid he spends too much time with his cockerels.

Must stop now and do the washing, ironing, gardening and cooking while Sabrina is at school and Nelson is tied to his play-pen. We had to stop using the baby bouncer. His legs are so long, he kept hitting the ceiling.

No time for depression.

Love,

Vera

PS Retrieved the kangaroo book from the bin and experimented with 'braised gonads'. We found it more of a snack than a meal. Perhaps on a kangaroo, they are larger?

Dear DC Hogg,

You may have been puzzled by the string of
expletives left on your voice mail, but having
tried many times to contact you by telephone,
I'm afraid I was overcome by frustration.

I was calling on behalf of my old acquaintance, Irene Spencer, who claims she was being
plagued by a 'Mystery Man Stalker' before her
recent departure for Australia. I too have had
sightings of this 'Mystery Man' in my home
village of Little Shagthorne and am therefore in
a position to give you an unbiased description.
He is tall, in the prime of life (about forty) with
a youthful complexion, golden locks and a
lovely smile. Far from being threatening, he is
kind and chivalrous. Indeed, I was rescued by
him from an unfortunate accident. If it hadn't
been for his prompt action I might have
languished at the bottom of a muddy pit for
days, my cries unheeded by callous, drunken
builders.

I long to meet him again, when not concussed. But, like a prince in a fairy tale, he
disappeared before I could thank him. I understand (though one has to take everything Irene

says with a pinch of salt) he has been sighted back in Hethergreen? If you can fit reading this letter and apprehending him into your busy schedule, I'd like to be the first to know.

Do, please, contact me at the above address if I can be of further assistance.

Yours very sincerely,

Vera Small

Dear Vera, Karen, St John, little Sabrina, Baby Boy Nelson, Howard and Anthony,

Rejoice, rejoice! My daughter Lesley is finally engaged to be married to Mr Brian Benbow of St Urban, Melbourne!

Excitedly yours,

Proud Mum Irene xxxxxxxxx

Dear Irene,

Penning a quick notelet while waiting for
Karen to come round from anaesthetic. She was
safely delivered of a little girl at 4.00 am this
morning. St John was woken at 2.00 am by an
emergency call and we rushed to the hospital to
watch them perform a Caesarian section.
Fascinating! Karen made a great fuss, howling
and thrashing, and when St John offered her his
hand, she bit it. I pointed out to her that it
would be a great deal worse if she had to go
through proper labour. As it was, the triage
nurse gave her an injection which knocked her
out, and all she has to deal with are a few
stitches. As the baby is so premature, she was
taken straight to an incubator (fortunately they
still have them in the private wing). She's
absolutely sweet, though very small, not a bit
like Nelson!

So, my dear, we both have reason to celebrate.
I'm so pleased for you that Lesley is engaged at
last. I've read between the lines and know that
with your straight-laced views, you found the
situation there humiliating and embarrassing.
When, exactly, are they getting married?

Anyway, St John, Howard and I send congratulations, as will Karen when she surfaces. Oh, I can hear some stirrings from the bed . . .

It was just Karen demanding another injection. I managed to tell her Lesley's news, but all she said was 'poor cow'. When I asked her if she'd thought of an appropriate new millennial name for the baby, she muttered, 'F*** the f***ing millennium'. Of course she's still very groggy. If she sticks to it, we'll call the little scrap 'Millie'.

Lots of love from all of us to all of you, xx

Vera

Congratulations, Granny Small – you've done it again!

Lesley's wedding 13th of next month. I'm so excited. You're all invited. Would love to have you over to help with the catering, if Karen can spare you?

Lots of love,

Irene x

On the Birth of your New Baby

by
Irene Spencer

Congratulations, Karen dear,
Sing Ho! Sing Hi! Sing Hay!
For unto you is born a girl
This bright and sunny day.

May blessings fall upon your heads
And all your dreams come true,
These flowers and these kisses are
With love, from me to you.

Irene xx

Vera,

Wedding off. Don't come. Am in despair.

Irene

Dear Irene,

I'm so excited about your daughter's wedding in Australia too! Every time I look at 'vera'svoyages' on my e-mail address, I think it's high time I went on another one. I could certainly do with a break from The Bothy. I work fourteen hours without even the minimum wage. Gone are the days when being over sixty meant welcome retirement!

My daughter Karen won't be able to come, much as she'd like to, as she has to stay and express milk for little Millie, who is still in the incubator. Karen is grumbling that she's nothing but a milking machine. Her husband St John can't take the time off and my grandson Nelson is far too much of a handful, so it will be just me and my granddaughter Sabrina. I'll have to get a full-fare ticket for her, she's so tall and tomboyish you won't recognise her! Hope I'll be able to persuade her out of her football boots for the wedding . . .

Later:

Have searched the World Wide Web for travel arrangements and come up with bomb.com which is offering flights at miraculously low prices.

All being well, Sabrina and I will be with you on the 10th, in good time for me to give you a hand with the catering. In the meantime, I've attached a favourite recipe. You should be able to get the ingredients and it's ever so easy. Even for an amateur.

Lots of love,

Vera

Curried Bananas
Bananas
Ginger wine
Garlic
Chilli powder

Marinate bananas overnight, then pop in the oven for 20 mins, or, if you're feeling brave, flambé!

Dear Lesley,

Gutted I won't be at your wedding. I was really looking forward to a good piss-up, and sneaking off for a snog with the best man (whoever that is). Ma absolutely refuses to let me come on the grounds that the bloody baby 'needs me'. Don't know why. The bloody deep-freeze is stacked with milk already.

Are you sure you know what you're doing? I said keep the ring, not Brian!

Anyway, lots of luck, girl,

Karen

Dear Karen,

What are you going on about? I *have* kept the ring and dumped Brian. Mum's going demented about it (so what else is new?).

Lesley x

Vera!

Didn't you get my last e-mail? I said the wedding's *off* and not to come! Don't tell me you've bought your tickets already or I'll never forgive myself.

Reply immediately marked URGENT. I need to know whether to worry or not.

Yours in desperation of new-fangled methods of so-called communication,

Irene

<u>URGENT</u>

Dear Irene,

No, I didn't get your last e-mail – are you sure it wasn't in your returned mail? My recipe-book proposal came back saying 'service undeliverable'. So, taking advantage of the remarkable discounts offered on the net, I booked and paid for the plane tickets. Needless to say, bomb.com won't consider a refund. Besides, Sabrina would be terribly disappointed. It will be her first experience of a plane and she's so looking forward to it.

I'm sure it's not Brian who's called it off, after all he's promised. Don't you think your daughter Lesley's just having an attack of pre-wedding jitters? She probably needs a good talking to about shouldering her responsibilities and I'm sure, between us, we can deliver it. There's baby 'Bubbles' to consider, to say nothing of the trouble and expense all her guests have been to. I've spent a fortune on a hyacinth-pink silk two-piece with matching 'petal' hat. Of course, I'll get the wear out of it on my next Dales TV appearance, but still . . .

So we'll be with you on the 10th as planned. I shall 'copy and paste' this into my letter format now and put it in the post, to be absolutely sure you get it. You're quite right – no matter how despised by 'modernisers', the tried and trusted methods are best.

Love from us all, and a bracing thump for Lesley,

Vee

My Bedroom
Byron St
St Urban
Melbourne
Australia

Dear Vera,

By the time you read this, *you* will be sitting
here in my bedroom, and I will be on a plane
back to Blighty. Tried e-mailing and phoning to
stop you, but you'd already left Little
Shagthorne. Why on earth did you think it
would take you two days to get to the airport?
I've heard of leaving in plenty of time, but
really . . .

Have had an absolute bombshell dropped into
my life – see attached letter from Beryl-next-
door in Hethergreen. She always goes in to
water the plants when I'm away, and to switch
lights on and off and open and close curtains in
a stimulation of me being in residence. Don't
know what I'm going to walk into when I get
back – my poor little house! *Now* tell me I was
over-reacting about the Mystery Man Stalker if
you dare! But character judgement has never
been your greatest strength.

No time now – am flinging things in suitcase
as I write, hence the scribble. Make yourself
completely at home while you're here. What's
mine is yours, as you know, which most likely, if

I know my daughter Lesley, will mean full childcare duties and all housekeeping, cleaning and cooking. See if you can drum some sense into her about marrying Brian, and feel absolutely free to deliver that 'bracing thump' you mentioned in your last.

Ill wind – had a small win on Tattslotto this week (Australia's national lottery), so will be buying myself a computer when I pass through Koala Lumpur Duty-Free on my way home. Will let you know my new e-mail address, and you should get Lesley to give you one while you're here.

Love to Sabrina. Little Cheryl Marie is dying to meet her.

More soon.

In haste and trepidation,

Irene

PS Paid for Creative Writing Course at St Urbans Community Centre in full, and five lessons left. Go in my stead if you want to. Tuesdays at three.

Dear Irene,

I'm ever so sorry to tell you you've been broken into. I was taken badly again and had to go into hospital for a couple of days with my bottom, so wasn't doing the usual with the curtains and lights. Got back to a bombsite.

Police got your door boarded up – it had been kicked in. Your telly's gone and your video, but I can't tell what else as it's such a mess. Am sending you the red notice from the boarder-uppers – they've been round in person to try to get their money from me, but I couldn't afford to pay them on my pension. Apparently they get let down a lot what with police calling them in and then people not paying, so their new company policy is to rip the boarding down again if they don't get their money within a week. Can you come home? Otherwise I may as well put a notice up over your door telling people to help themselves, let alone the weather coming into your lounge.

Haven't told you the worst. That chap who I've seen hanging around, and who roked through your dustbin that time, was seen running off after the break-in, by Betty Slapper up the street. Last night, coming home from bingo, I saw him and screamed 'Burglar!'

Instead of running away, he came over, bold as brass, and said to tell you he's got your stuff in safe-keeping. Have told police, and they're waiting for a ransom notice. They're flummoxed. They've never heard of a telly being kidnapped before.

Can you bring me Cherry Brandy from Duty-Free? I've gone off Midori.

Yours faithfully,

Beryl next door

Dear St John and Karen,

Amazed to arrive and find Irene already gone.
Rather put out after a three-day journey. No
wonder bomb.com were so insistent about
getting to the airport early, it was like a rugger
scrum to get on to the plane. Then we had to
wait while they put the door back on.

Irene had left a note insisting that she'd tried
to e-mail and phone about her change of plans,
but, as Lesley has subsequently confided, owing
to a recurrence of her old 'trouble', she is
getting increasingly forgetful. Apparently she is
now convinced that her Mystery Man Stalker
has broken into her home and stolen her video
for ransom purposes. It seems unlikely. It
wouldn't fetch more than a fiver at a boot fair,
but Irene dashed off in a flurry of high drama. I
await her next communication with dread.
Goodness knows what fanciful explanation she
will dream up.

In the meantime, Lesley has made us very
welcome. What a charming girl she is, not a bit
like Irene's descriptions of her. I can see exactly
why she doesn't want to marry Brian. He's fat
and bald and twenty years her senior. More
importantly, his dot com shares have taken a
nosedive and what with the alimony he has to
pay, he's unable to provide Lesley with any of

the promised comforts. She has kept the engagement ring, a large solitaire, and the hot tub in the garden. We've all had a lot of fun in that, though Sabrina does like to play rough with Cheryl Marie. Must stop, I can hear splashing and screaming from the garden.

Later:

Sabrina was holding Cheryl Marie's head under water again. Although they are the same age, Cheryl Marie is tiny and very feminine. And, of course, she wasn't brought up on a trailer park. Baby 'Bubbles' is going to be another little beauty. She's as good as her golden hair (she obviously doesn't get that from Brian!) and much less demanding than my grandson Nelson. Hope you're not finding looking after him too arduous, Karen. Still, you got plenty of rest lying on your back for a month in hospital.

All love,

Vee/Mother

Karen!

What the bloody hell is going on? Just got rid
of *my* Mum, and *yours* poles up to stay. Do
something!

Mum's found out she's been burgled at home
and was like a headless chicken till she left.
Couldn't stand it any more, so made some hash
cookies to calm her down. Course, she's one of
the tiny few it just makes hyper and paranoid
and I ended up wishing I hadn't bothered – she
was practically climbing the walls. Suppose I
should have learned my lesson last time she had
some of my dope by mistake and I had to put
her in the bin.

Seriously, if your Mother's thinking of staying
here, I'm coming over to you. I'd got a new
bloke I've been gagging for lined up for tonight,
and I thought at last I could bring him home.

Yours, demented (I swear to God it's
catching!),

Lesley

Dear Lesley, Vera, Cheryl Marie, Bubbles, and Sabrina,

How very odd to be writing to you all together! Arrived home in a chaos of emotion, having flown for twenty-four sleepless hours completely wide awake and rigid with tension. I don't even have to take my neck to Dr Shah tomorrow to know that she is going to have me under the physiotheraphist again with my lesions. The agony! Couldn't eat a thing on the plane – it all looked as if it would poison me. (Thank heavens for those delicious little 'Mary Warner' cakes you sent me off with, Lesley, otherwise I might have starved. You must show the recipe to Vera and see if she wants to include it in her book.) Man (wearing gloves) sitting next to me on plane had a black leather attaché case under his seat, and he kept leaving it and going off to the loo. Couldn't get the air hostess to take me seriously when I told her I suspected it was a bomb, so had to sit there completely immobile for the whole flight for fear of setting it off.

Got here, wrung out, dreading worst, finding the inexplicable. Too tired to go into it now but wanted to let you have my new e-mail address. Bought smashing little laptop, marvellous price – thoroughly recommend Chung Chang's

Cheap Computers in Koala Lumpur Duty-Free.

Must sleep. Can't go on any longer. Would love to tell you of miracle and coming home to dream instead of nightmare but am still feeling strange. So good to have the blood back in my legs though – I could feel the benefit as soon as we were the right side of the equator. How are you with being upside-down and it all having rushed to your head, Vera?

Got to stop. Eyes closing. Neck like red hot poker.

Love,

Irene/Mum/Granny ZZZZZZ

Dear Irene,

The blood certainly rushed to my head on receipt of an e-mail from my son-in-law St John. My daughter Karen has absconded with the triage nurse. Poor little Millie is an abandoned child before she is out of the incubator! Don't talk to me about 'chaos of emotion'! St John, with his schedule, has to rush to the hospital several times a day to feed the poor little mite with expressed breast milk. I only hope he remembers to defrost it. Baby Nelson has had to be farmed out to my son Howard and his partner Antony at Sheepdipper's Shed. Goodness knows how they'll manage with a herd of sheep as well. Looking after Nelson is a full-time job. Still, I suppose it will be good practice for when they get their own baby.

As you can imagine, I was pole-axed. But lovely Lesley came to the rescue. She said much as she would miss me, I was obviously needed at home straight away. She rushed around organising flights, has done all our packing and is now in the kitchen baking some 'Mary Warner' cakes for the journey. She says to send you her love and tell you she'll give me the recipe.

I'm sorry to be going so soon, I was just getting used to being 'topsy-turvy'. I'd even

124

dropped in to your creative writing class. I didn't stay. I flicked through some of the work on show and let's just say I can see where you get your expressions.

Lesley has persuaded a charming young male friend to give us a lift to the airport. We leave for the flight at 5.00 am upside-down time. Next time mail me at 'littleshag'.

Love, except I'll probably never feel it again, especially for Karen,

Vera

Dear Lesley,

Well, you did say 'Do something'!

Love,

Karen

Dear Vera,

Trust you are safely ensconed back at Little Shagthorne now and have taken control of the family situation. Has anybody heard from your daughter Karen yet? Imagine being able to abandon a newborn baby! She must be completely distraught about *something* – she's normally such a lovely girl. I find it hard to believe that she is in any kind of romantic entanglement with the triage nurse who disappeared with her – he's a friend of your son Howard and his partner Antony's, isn't he, so surely he's of the other persuasion. Perhaps they've just gone shopping?

I have been having shock after shock back home in Hethergreen. I returned, as you know, expecting to find mayhem after Beryl-next-door's letter telling me about the break in, and instead I found everything looking lovely. The front door had been put back on its hinges, everywhere had been hoovered and dusted, and there was the most wonderful flower arrangement from 'Flora's Tributes' (very posh florist in nearby Monkston Magna). Naturally I assumed it was Beryl I had to thank, so imagine my surprise, not to mention utter discombobulation, when I took her Cherry Brandy round to thank her and she said that all she had done was to let the cleaners in. 'What cleaners?' I hear you ask, as indeed did I. 'The cleaners you arranged to come in and tidy up,' she said (she's a nice woman, but very simple). 'But I sent no cleaners!' said I. And Vera, I didn't.

I've e-mailed your son-in-law St John, as it's just the sort of kind thing he would arrange, but he replied saying it wasn't him (he does sound lost without Karen – do please give him a motherly hug from me). I've been all round the village asking, but nobody knows a thing. I even e-mailed Edward Blunt, our one time would-be poultry-farming paramour, wondering if he might perhaps be refining his seduction techniques, but he just sent me a foul reply (if you'll forgive the pun) saying that cleaning is what women are for (I won't pass on what he went on to say that men are supposed to be for, but suffice it to say it's nothing useful in the housekeeping department).

I am now left with the unlikely scenearia that I was broken into and burgled by the Mystery Man Stalker who Beryl saw hanging around my back entrance, and then cleaned up again by 'person or persons unknown', as DC Hogg has filed in his report. My TV and video are still missing, as is, most upsettingly, my wedding photo. Why would they want that, other than to be hurtful? They'd get nothing for it – the frame wasn't even antique. I told you, didn't I, that Beryl saw the Mystery Man on her way back from bingo, and he told her he had my things in 'safe-keeping'. Since this is the most dramatic crime Hethergreen has ever known, CID have 'wired' me for sound, and I am supposed to go about my business wearing a little microphone in my lapel and a battery pack strapped to my thigh in case he approaches me. It makes walking very awkward, and crossing my legs an impossibility. And it's all very well for Hogg and his associates to get excited about it (they keep talking about offering to meet him in a field in just their underpants – what is it about men?), but I feel like a lonely little lamb who's been put out as a lure for the big bad wolf. I carry a Jif lemon with me now, wherever I go, in case of attack.

Anyway, dear, enough about me and my worries. Poor you, going all the way to Australia and then having to turn round and come straight back – you must be exhausted. Not to mention being terrified about the welfare of your missing daughter. If there's anything I can do to help find her, particularly now that I am 'wired for sound', don't hesitate to let me know.

But for all our worries, isn't it nice to be back home in Blighty?

Much love,

Irene x

Dear Irene,

I'm sorry to have been a while replying, but
what with unpacking, washing, cleaning and the
computer being down – something about a
brown ale being spilled on it – everything's
been more 'topsy-turvy' since I got back than
when I was in Australia. Far from the cleaners
having been in, the whole of The Bothy was
strewn with takeaway cartons, empty beer
bottles and cigarette butts. Which is odd as St
John isn't a smoker. There were discarded
clothes everywhere, all the beds had been used
and the sheets and pillows thrown all over the
place. Quite honestly, if it had been anyone but
St John, I'd suspect there'd been an orgy. His
explanation is that he didn't have time to
change the beds, so just took it in turns to sleep
in them. A mother-in-law's job is never done
and, jet-lagged as I was, I had to get straight to
the hoovering.

Fortunately the return journey was a lot faster
with 'Ripper No-Frills Airline'. Which was just
as well, as they took 'no-frills' to the limit and
didn't provide any lavatories or sustenance. I'd
just popped the last 'Mary Warner' cake into my
mouth – they really are delicious, I'll be trying
out the recipe – when we put down in Dubai
for a stopover in their fabulous Duty-Free. I

wandered, entranced by the multi-coloured garments and mouth-watering scents, and found myself buying a cornucopia of presents. My granddaughter Sabrina got a David Beckham football cap complete with streaked-blond, floppy hair 'extensions' (she thought it looked funny perched on top of her head, but, as I pointed out, no funnier than it used to do on his), while I stocked up on the exotic foods and herbs I didn't have chance to buy in St Urban. With enough tots at home to open a nursery, I went completely overboard on the 'designer' baby clothes. They had the most marvellous accessories as well, and I couldn't resist some fluffy pale pink and blue pashminas. My son Howard and his partner Antony claimed them both straight away on the grounds that their baby-to-be might be either sex, but later I saw them wearing them in Great Shagthorne Tesco's.

No word at all from Karen and the boys are absolutely mystified. Howard's convinced that their friend Brett, the triage nurse she's run off with, is anything but 'straight' and what's more, he's got the photos to prove it. Apparently, the local tourist board has been running a campaign to promote Great Shagthorne as the gay capital of the Dales and as part of a Mardi Gras weekend, Dales TV ran a 'Take Home A Tranny' competition. Brett took first prize impersonating Posh Spice, wearing a mini-slip he'd made himself from fifty-pound notes. As Howard said, goodness knows how he managed that on the pay of a triage nurse.

I've taken over the care of my granddaughter, little Millie, now she's allowed out of the incubator for a few hours. Antony's made her a darling little sheepskin papoose and it's the envy of all the other mothers. In fact, such has been the demand that Antony's thinking of going into business. Now he and Howard have got their own baby on the way, they could do with a regular money-spinner. Life on a sheep farm has its ups and downs financially, as Dales TV's 'A Life With Sheep' has documented. Still, at least they're intimate with the raw materials.

Have just come back from a brisk trot in the hospital grounds with baby Millie on my back, pit bull terrier Rex on his lead and grandson Nelson in his push-chair. At this rate, I'll never need to take up Yoga!

The boys are coming over for a pow-wow on the situation tonight, so must now stop and light the paraffin stove. I'm trying out a new recipe for my cookery book, 'Ginger and Lemon Grass with Home-Smoked Alligator'.

I do hope you've solved the Hethergreen Mysteries – sounds like one for your 'creative writing' course, doesn't it? I'm sure you don't miss the wedding photo, but you must be lost without your TV and video.

Mail me soon with the next instalment, I'm hooked.

Love,

Vera

PS Do beware while you're 'wired for sound'. Who on earth's on the other end when you're spending a penny?

Dear Vera,

Thank you for your long and newsy e-mail, albeit tardy. I had to get my dictionary out to understand half of what you were on about, and even now I am none the wiser for its hallucidation. What *is* a pashmina? You mentioned them before when you were in India, and I thought at the time perhaps it might be something to eat, given that that seems to be your preoccupation these days, but now I'm not so sure, as you say Howard and Antony have been *wearing* them to do the shopping.

Likewise, 'tranny', which I always thought was slang for transistor radio – I remember that Lesley nagged us all through her teen years for one. Couldn't find it in the dictionary, so asked Beryl-next-door, and she said it's somebody like Danny La Rue. So let me get this straight – your gay son Howard says that his sister Karen has run off with Brett the triage nurse who likes to wear ladies' dresses . . . ? Is it just me, or is there something funny about that?

Last, but not least, in the incomprehension stakes, I looked up 'papoose', which apparently is the name for a Red Indian baby – although we're supposed to call them Native Americans now, of course. So Antony has made a baby out of sheepskin for little Millie, and is thinking it could be a money-spinner. Didn't we used to call them dolls – or teddy bears perhaps?

No sign so far of the Mystery Man. I'm feeling a bit exposed because Beryl-next-door's back in hospital with her bottom (don't ask – I did, and honestly, after a two-hour monologue I was *heaving*), so if he did appear, there would be nobody to hear my screams. I know I'm supposed to be 'wired for sound', but it only works when I switch it on otherwise the battery would run out, and the knob is in such an awkward position – I told you it's strapped to the inside of my thigh, didn't I? Frankly, I don't know how I'm supposed to turn it on casually without him noticing, while engaging him in conversation long enough for the police to respond. I mean, what would *you* think if a woman my age started fiddling up her skirt when she was talking to you? (Don't feel you have to answer that, Vera – it was a retortical question.)

Insurance won't pay up for a replacement TV and video because they say they aren't stolen but kidnapped, so my evenings are very long at the moment. The radio is all very nice of course, but it doesn't lull you into a stupor the same way as the telly, does it?

I do hope your son-in-law St John isn't playing fast and loose while Karen is missing. It's all very well him saying he kept switching beds, but the cigarette ends just don't add up, do they, if he's not a smoker? And what will happen to you if she never comes back? Rare is the man who would have his mother-in-law living with him if she didn't come as part of the bridal package. Still, I suppose he'll keep you while you're useful to him, looking after the children.

Anyway, dear, keep your chin up. Lots of love,

Irene x

Dear Lesley,

Don't let on to the old dears but I'm staying with Brett and his boyfriend. I ran away to punish St John. It was bad enough him forcing me to be 'healthy' while I'm breast-feeding, but when I got home I found suspicious signs and made him admit; over a bowl of bloody sheep's yoghurt, that he'd been having an affair while I was in hospital. Don't know who with, except, judging by the empty tinnies and fag ends in the trash bags, she's a chain-smoking alcoholic. God knows how Ma didn't notice, but she only sees what she wants to where he's concerned. Anyway, I chucked the yoghurt over his head and I'm not going home until the bastard grovels.

Brett says I'm suffering from post-natal depression, but fortunately he can lay his hands on just the substances to sort it! Having a high time. Hope you are too.

Karen

Dear Irene,

In haste as we are in the midst of another
crisis. Howard and Antony's baby-mother,
Natasha, has just arrived in tears, having been
thrown out by her husband! I'm not surprised,
I always thought he must be an odd man to
allow her to do the job in the first place.
Goodness knows why she came here instead of
Sheepdipper's. I can only think she feels she has
more of a relationship with St John. Or at least
with his syringe. Incidentally, despite your
unpleasant aspidersions, St John has explained,
perfectly reasonably, that the mess at The Bothy
was as the result of a Dales TV 'wrap' party.

More when I can think beyond extra bedding,

Vera

Vera!

Get off the phone, or stop scurfing the Web or whatever it is you're doing! I need to speak to you urgently!

Was dead-heading the flower arrangement from 'person or persons unknown' and found a card nestling in the petals, which I had hitherto overlooked. It says 'Dear Mrs Spencer, Trust you find everything as you left it, minus the TV and video of course. I shall call to see you on Tuesday afternoon at 4.00 pm, when I hope we will have a pleasant meeting to our mutual advantage. Yours truly, C. Thorogood'.

I can't get DC Hogg on the phone either and I'm at my wits' end since it's five-to-four already. Help me!!!!!!!!!!

Too late. He's ringing the doorbell. I shall stay very quiet and not answer. Oh no! He's looking through the letterbox straight at me . . . If there's no reply when you phone, call Hogg and tell him to track down C. Thorogood immediately!

Yours desperately,

Irene

Irene!

Have rung and rung as instructed in your last, but just get the engaged signal. Tried the operator – some cretin in a call centre – and eventually, after being re-routed via Glasgow, Milton Keynes and, for all I know, another planet, discovered your phone is off the hook. My mind raced far and wide over the possibilities. Perhaps you're involved in a romantic encounter during which you don't welcome disturbance. I dismissed that one immediately. Or maybe a struggle took place where the phone was dislodged, and you are, as I write, gagged and bound to a kitchen chair. If I recall correctly, your phone is in the kitchen, in which case that dreadful buzz it makes when it's off the hook must be adding to your discomfort. Worst of all, you may have been murdered and are now lying, strangled with your 'wire' or with blood gushing from a fatal wound, at the foot of your stairs. On second thoughts it couldn't be the stairs, I've just remembered you live in a bungalow.

You'll be glad to know this all rushed through my brain at the pace of what my granddaughter Sabrina calls a 'nano-second' and I was straight away on the phone to DC Hogg demanding he send in the Instant Response Unit. As usual he had his 'voice mail' on – I suppose it *is* tea-time – but I left a message he won't forget in a hurry.

Dear, dear friend, how sorry I am you live so far away, otherwise I would dash straight round myself, with a dose of my veterinarian son-in-law St John's animal tranquilliser. It has, as you know, proved a life-saver on previous occasions.

Hope this reaches you and does not merely languish in your e-mail 'inbox' until a social worker finds it. Please let me know AT ONCE what is happening! I'm sitting at the computer with everything crossed and am in agony with cramp all over.

Vee

Dear Vera,

Have finally recovered from the smoke bomb and finished clearing up the house with Christopher's help – what on *earth* did you say to DC Hogg's voice mail? Whatever it was, he was taking no prisoners. There we were, getting to know each other over a cup of tea and Fondant Fancies, when a troupe of uniformed officers in riot gear and breathing apparatus bashed down the door with a battering ram without even bothering to knock first, exploded some device that had us both choking and blinded, and when the smoke finally cleared and our eyes managed to re-open, there was Hogg, in his underpants, standing in the doorway waving his truncheon. Naturally I shall be lodging a formal complaint. The phone wasn't so much 'off the hook' as ripped out of the wall. They caused absolute mayhem trampling through the living room, turning over furniture and throwing things about. My weeping fig will certainly never be the same again. Still, I'm sure you meant well.

All for now, as Chris is picking me up in a minute in his Jaguar to take me out to dinner, but thought I'd better let you know I'm still alive. Just.

Best wishes,

Irene

Dear Irene,

I'm sorry, I'm sure, if my prompt action on your behalf has caused offence, but your hysteria left me no option. As to the message I left for DC Hogg, at least it seems to have done the trick and got him off his voice mail. I didn't bother mentioning stalkers and flashers but went straight to 'armed guerilla' and 'hostage situation'. I reminded him of the calumny that nowadays falls on police officers who are perceived to have failed in their duty towards vulnerable minorities – in this case the aged – and conversely how we celebrate those who take a stand, albeit in their underpants. I may even have mentioned a knighthood. Your own instant response is, as usual, to misunderstand and misjudge the blameless motives of a true friend. Really, the phrase 'dog in the manger' could have been invented for you.

Which reminds me, with all the drama I may have forgotten to tell you that Rex, my pit bull terrier, was shot last week by your ex-paramour Edward Blunt, who claimed the poor little pooch was 'worrying' his chickens. I imagine they have more to 'worry' about from Edward himself . . . but that's another story. St John had to operate at once to remove sixteen pellets of buckshot from Rex's gut, before it went to gangrene. As if that isn't enough, there have been terrible scenes between St John, my son Howard and his partner Antony, and Natasha, their surrogate mother. No one will tell me what is going on and when I pressed Howard, who usually confides everything, he burst into tears and rushed away, sobbing something about 'St John's bloody insemination'. I've never heard him complain before, they've always been more than satisfied with the sheep-flock's breeding record. The last row kept me awake 'til five o'clock this morning. It can't be good for Natasha when she's pregnant. She's moved into my daughter Karen's West Wing turret. Temporarily.

Well, Irene, I'm relieved to know you're all right, but whom or what is this 'Christopher'? Is he the mystery stalker? You give no explanation and yet, after your alarmist missive, here you are on first name terms, sharing Fondant Fancies. Were you 'wired for sound' throughout the encounter? In which case, if you are too engrossed with dinner parties, you can simply send me the tape.

Must stop. Rex has slipped his surgical restraint and is tearing round the garden after Sabrina's pet ferret.

Love and good luck,

Vera

Dear Vera,

Who is 'Christopher' indeed. Well, he is many things. Marvellous things. Heroic things. And, also, things of a personal nature which are very difficult to talk about. Where to start?

Well, first, with the mystery of the kidnapped television and video. There I was, away from home in Australia, as you will remember, staying with the girl who calls me 'Mother' but who treats me like a slave, and Christopher, not knowing this, had come round to see me here at The Limes. He couldn't help noticing as he was walking up the path that there was a gaping hole where my front door used to be, and just as he was puzzling out why that might be, two boys ran out of it, knocking him to the ground and making off with my electrical goods. Thinking naught of his own safety, he immediately gave chase and miraculously caught up with them (but then he is not only very handsome but also extremely fit) in Bolsover Close. It turned out that they were *children* of barely ten years, so instead of turning them over to the police (he is also a wonderfully kind person), he confiscated their 'booty' and gave them a very severe talking to. However, (since he is also very intelligent and sensible) on returning the stolen artefacts to my house, he deduced from my packing list which I'd left on the table, and from the note I had left for Beryl-next-door about the proper watering of my amaryllis (she murdered my peace lily last time I was away), that I was not currently in residence, so he took them to his own home for safe-keeping. Beryl, as we know, saw him leaving with them, didn't hear what he was telling her (she's become so hard of hearing you really have to *scream* at her, with hand signals, these days to know that you've effectively got through), and she jumped to the erroniatious conclusion that he was stealing them himself and holding them to ransom, hence all the misunderstandings. He *did* take my wedding photo, of course, which was the only likeness of me that he saw on display in my living room, but only to make a copy of it for himself – he's returned the original to me safe and sound. He it was who organised for the cleaners to go in, so that my homecoming would be trauma-free.

Yes, he is the 'Mystery Man Stalker'. He has been wanting to meet me for some time, but was afraid to make himself known by letter (he is also supremely sensitive) for fear of upsetting me when he wasn't there to deal personally with the consequences. He had been following me merely in the hope of introducing himself at an opportune moment, but unfortunately one never arose. He even tracked me down to The Bothy when I was staying there in lieu of you, which is how he came to pull you out of the swimming pool, but of course, by then I'd left.

Now we come to the difficult part, which I can barely bring myself to write. That which I have kept secret for so long I now feel like shouting from the rooftops, for out of darkest shame has come shining glory – but the habit of silence and guilt runs deep, and I, poet and creative writer that I am, am almost lost for words . . .

You may have noticed during the time that you have known me that I value, above all things, duty, obedience, and responsibility. That is how I was brought up. To say that my mother and father were 'strict' is to say that the Spanish Inquisition just wanted to get to the facts . . . I can't go on in prose form. I need the subtle nuance of verse.

The Ballad of Irene Spencer

by
Irene Spencer

Once, there was a young, young girl,
of barely seventeen,
Who strived to be a credit, by keeping
herself clean.
Alas, there was an accident; alas she
'caught her toe',

For there were things in heaven and earth that
she really didn't know –
Of how the birds and bees were made, of the
mysteries of life
And, ignorance being no defence, her parents
gave her strife.

They wouldn't listen when she said
It wasn't her but their friend Fred –
That he had thrown her on the bed
And sin had reared its ugly head,
That she had begged, polite at first,
But he had merely laughed and cursed,
And as he was doing his wicked worst,
What he called 'protection' had gone and burst.

Do not judge me, unlike them,
Or think that I was crude,
For there hasn't been a day since then
That I have not wept and rued
That a baby grew inside my tummy
Who never got to call me Mummy
For he was taken from my side
As soon as he was washed and dried.

Perhaps you have guessed it, Vera. Christopher
is my son, and he has found me at last.
Yours, in a curious, heady, admixture of
shame and unbridled excitement,

Irene

Dear Irene,

You think you've got Drama, Shame and Guilt? We've had enough here to fill a novel by Dosto-evsky. Sadly I can't resort to versifying – and I must say your last had all the subtle nuance of the Encyclopaedia Britannica – so I will just enumerate the brutal facts.

My daughter Karen turned up in the middle of the night and found her husband St John up the turret with Natasha.

My son Howard and his partner Antony's baby is actually St John's.

Howard and Antony aren't speaking to St John.

Karen thumped Natasha.

I discovered my granddaughter Sabrina 'begging' outside her school at Little Shagthorne. She had her brother Nelson in his stroller, Rex on a string and the lollipop lady, Brenda, in a head-lock. I'm afraid I lost control and slapped her. She slapped me back and shouted she'd already made £5 and I was a stupid c-word to stop her. This, I suppose, is the famed 'language of the playground'. You talk about the tragedy of our childhoods, but, I ask you, with all this modern so-called 'enlightenment' and 'political correctness', are things really any better?

All this, just as Dales TV is about to air the

first episode of our documentary 'A Life With Sheep'. There was supposed to be a 'Do' round here to celebrate it. But with nobody on speaking terms and Howard and Antony constantly in tears, a wake would be more appropriate.

I'm sorry, my dear, I haven't even commented on your astounding news. You must be on cloud nine. And to think, I was the first to perceive Christopher's wonderful qualities. I look forward to meeting him again, now he's officially 'family'. What am I saying? More family is the last thing either of us needs! Maybe you should just be friends with him?

All my love,

Vee

PS A word of advice, Irene, *as* a friend. Don't get any ideas about lashing out in the novel form. I'm sorry I mentioned Dosto-evsky.

Dear Vera,

So grateful that you could spare the time from the vivid saga of your 'problem' family (it must take you back to your days in the trailer park) to congratulate me on being reunited with my son after all these years.

I am sorry that recent events in your own life have turned you against 'the family'. Personally, I am more than delighted currently to be wrapped in the bosom of my own. By the by, did I mention that my daughter Lesley is getting married after all? Christopher and I are planning to fly out to Melbourne together for the wedding (Club Class – his treat). I'd invite you to come along and help with the catering, but you must already be up to your armpits in the stew you're in at the moment, so I won't add to your burdens.

Take care, my dear.

With love from your blissfully happy and fulfilled friend,

Irene

Dear Irene,

I'm a star! 'A Life With Sheep' is a big hit.
Karen and St John are re-united – it's a long
story, more when I have time off from dealing
with all my congratulatory e-mails – Dales TV
has never had so many, and they all said how
empatholic I was! Natasha has gone to live with
Howard and Antony until her baby is born. The
boys plan to 'hothouse' it (whatever *that*
means!) in the womb, despite having no luck
with the grapevines. They're already playing it
Abba hits. They've been approached by a multi-
national organisation wanting to turn Sheepdipper's into a Theme Park. At last their future
is secure! As the programme showed, it's
obviously not in sheep farming.

Best of all, I've been invited by Dales TV to
host my own morning programme! A magazine
with a daily recipe insert. Perfect! Have a
wonderful time in Oz, I'm far too busy to come
anyway.

Love to you all,

Vera

PS Dales TV say with my ebullient personality,
it would be good if I had a foil, someone less
colourful and vibrant. So, when you return from
Oz, how about it . . . ?